$ECRET HABIT$

OF

$UCCE$$FUL BA$TARD$

The self-help book for people who are too nice to ever be successful

Adrian Maile

www.successful-bastards.com

Published 2007

by

SB Publishing

PO Box 61628
London
SE12 0XS

Copyright © Adrian Maile 2007

I dedicate this book to me.

I am proud to be a self-made successful bastard and I need thank nobody but myself.

There is a little bit of the bastard in all of us, but most people are afraid to be a bastard when they need to be.

Most successful people have no qualms about being a bastard and are more successful because of that.
You wish you could be more like them, don't you?

This book:

✓ Will change your mind about what you have to do to be successful

✓ Will open opportunities for success beyond your wildest dreams

✓ Have you laughing all the way to the bank.

You will learn:

✓ Just how much of a bastard you and others are

✓ How to exploit your limited talents and resources to be successful in the real world

- ✓ Why being nice gets you nowhere

- ✓ The secret behaviours that successful bastards use to get wealthy, powerful and happy:

- ✓ 20 ways to be more of a bastard when you need to be

- ✓ 100 techniques to apply to make you a more powerful, wealthy and successful bastard

- ✓ When to ease off and how to get out of trouble

- ✓ That you can be a bastard and be very happy and well-liked.

You will have fun:

- ✓ Realising the absurdity of how being more of a bastard will make you more popular and successful

- ✓ Measuring your progress on the Bastard-o-meter

- ✓ Measuring how much of a bastard other people are

- ✓ Reading about how famously successful bastards really made their fortunes.

CONTENTS

Foreword

"The object of war is not to die for your country, but to make the other bastard die for his." General George Patten

I was born in 1962, on the 24th of March. Mark that date in your diary and send me a birthday card every year. Send it to my publisher, marked for my attention and it will find its way to me. My publisher is good like that.

If you add your name and address I will add you to my fan-club mailing list and you can make your first connection to the exclusive club where only successful bastards are members. You never know when we might be able to help each other.

If you think that I seem a little selfish, you would be wrong. I am very selfish and so should you be. I look after myself, like William Aldinger III, the chief executive at an American Bank that was acquired by HSBC, who despite a pay deal worth £37M demanded it include free dental treatment, for him and his wife, *for life* and personal use of the Corporate jet, to continue even should he be fired. HSBC could not calculate how much it would cost to fire him so he got what he wanted and so will I. Get your diary out now and make the note, before you forget.

I am also very lazy and greedy and proud of it. If Andrew Carnegie, once the richest man in the world, managed to get fabulously wealthy working just three hours a day, six months of the year and travelling the world socialising, self-indulging and scribbling how-to-get-rich books the other six, so can I. There may well be workers' blood on my hands, like there was on his, but I will wash them before I leave the office.

As you can probably guess I like giving direct orders. It works. I can be rude, argumentative and aggressive and I fear nothing. My bark is as bad as my bite. I operate like that famously once successful, now dead, bastard Lord Robert Maxwell. Like him, when I walk into a room, people mutter, "The Ego Has Landed." Short barked orders and telephones hung up before calls have finished work for me as they did for him. One major difference between us is that I will not fail and have to mysteriously drown myself so the wife gets the insurance money, the kids take the blame and I get to be buried in Holy Land after a full-blown state-funeral. I will not fail.

I am also pretty damn ruthless and unforgiving. If I find out you read this book and did not send me a birthday card, I will be displeased. If you cannot follow simple instructions you are clearly worthless to me and a person who deserves some punishment. I may react like the multi-millionaire property baron Nicholas van Hoogstraten who sent the boys around to a former business partner's house and they ended up killing him.

$ecret Habit$ of $ucce$$ful Ba$tard$

Of course, I would appeal against the conviction for your manslaughter should it come to that and end up getting freed early just like van Hoogstraten did. How could I have foreseen that sending my henchmen around to your house would have ended in you getting stabbed five times and shot in the face before you died? I know I said I would add you to my fan club mailing list. I lied. I will not do that, somebody else will. I have got better things to do.

I also said that if you sent me that card, sometime in the future we might help each other. I lied again. I will not help you. I will just steal from you and profit from your ideas. You will not realise I am doing this, but if you do, it will probably be too late because I will wrap things up in complex legal challenges for years, should you decide to sue me. By the time it is all sorted out, my fortune will have been made.

Just like Bill Gates (Microsoft) and Larry Ellison (Oracle) and more recently Mark Zuckerberg (Facebook), the software billionaires who have all allegedly copied other people's ideas and used their resources without their knowledge and gone on to build giant businesses that have lined their pockets in the most spectacular way.

This book will change your mind about what you need to do to be successful. You thought it was hard work, intelligence and luck that made people successful. It is not. You have to be a bastard to be successful. You must be selfish, tough, ruthless and unpredictable – and I will show you how.

$ecret Habit$ of $ucce$$ful Ba$tard$

At first glance you might think the habits and techniques in this book are deplorable, painful to do and will result in people hating you. On the contrary, they will make you happier, wealthier and more successful and help you to build a wonderful circle of like-minded people around you.

You will discover friends you never dreamed you might have, famous and successful people that spring out of nowhere to admire you and a like-minded community of successful bastards who will be pleasantly surprised that you have joined their gang. Your social circle will increase dramatically and with it will come even more opportunities to build profitable associations with others and handsomely line your pockets.

If you know me and think you were an inspiration for my book in some way, you are probably wrong. Only a precious few can count themselves part of my success and I am not in the habit of giving other people compliments. My success has been self-made.

If you have read this far, I hope you have bought the book. I have been a bastard writing it and the royalties are rolling in. I am profiting because you, or whoever you stole it off, paid more for the book than it cost to produce.

I suppose I should thank you, but I will not. Why should I? You are getting more out of your copy than I gained from selling it to you.

$ecret Habit$ of $ucce$$ful Ba$tard$

The beauty of business is that this principle applies to everything. I am not exploiting you, you are getting a valuable service and thanks to selling lots of something that others produced cheaply on my behalf, I am getting rich in the process.

We will probably never meet if we have not already because I cannot be bothered to sign copies of this book to please a book retailer who is merely profiting at my expense but, if we do, please remember that I probably have more important things to do than stand and chat.

You have no one but yourself to blame if you do not get from life what you deserve. Be like me and squeeze every last drop of pleasure from yours.

Take care,

Adrian

"The person who has no enemies, has no followers." **Don Piatt**

Preface

"The power of accurate observation is frequently called cynicism by those who do not have it." **George Bernard Shaw**

Put your hand up if you think you <u>could</u> be more successful. Keep it up if you <u>want</u> to be more successful. If you have not got your hand up, close the book and put it back on the stand, shelf, coffee table or desk where you found it. Goodbye! Unless of course you were too self-conscious to put your hand up in the first place, in which case I suggest you read on. You need my help.

If you have got your hand up still, you can put it down now. Everyone in the shop, or wherever you are, probably wonders what you are doing anyway. I like the way you respond to direct orders. You are my kind of person, a nicely malleable one.

For those of you still with me, welcome. We probably do not know each other, which is probably good for both of us. If we do know each other, then you may well find yourself in here somewhere. Whether I know you, or not, I still know a lot about you. Let me tell you what I know.

I know that you would rather not work hard for a living. I know that despite this, you do work hard, bloody hard, nearly every bloody day. You work hard to make enough money to live. You struggle along and wish it were easier to make those distant ends meet. Most people do.

In the back of your mind, and as you have got older it has become front of mind more frequently, you plan to work hard to make enough money to retire early. If you are in your twenties, you plan it for when you are thirty-five. If you are in your thirties it is probably forty-five; forties - fifty, fifties – next year, sixties – next week. You would of course love to retire early so that you can enjoy retirement without needing a Zimmer frame or waterproof underwear and without having to get someone to liquidise your food for you. You dream of a long, healthy and wealthy, leisure filled rest period, sometime soon.

Like most people, however, you always run out of money before you run out of month and each month you postpone that early retirement one more month into the future. It happens so many times, month after month, and your early retirement plans slip so far into the future, that you forget about it for a while. That is normal. That is the way most people live in the 'civilised' world. They block all the shit out by keeping their heads firmly buried in the sand.

You take it for granted that life is a bitch, that it is supposed to be that way, and you plod on. Then, every month is the same and every month will continue to be the same, until you hit 60 or 65 and are forced to retire by your ungrateful employer or through ill-health, or you die. Life IS a bitch, no doubt about it. Sometimes, when your energy is high, you realise that if only you were just a bit more of a bastard, you might be able to take that bitch by the scruff of the neck and become just a little more successful in the process.

$ecret Habit$ of $ucce$$ful Ba$tard$

Every now and then, an opportunity presents itself for you to break the vicious circle of work and death and you dream of how you would enjoy it. Maybe you dream of being a 'fat-cat' business leader earning millions a year, or winning the lottery or some major competition prize. You dream of that perfect crime – robbing that Bank or embezzling your employer and never getting caught. Maybe you think that one day being your own boss will make you wealthy beyond belief, if only you could think of a good idea for a business or invent something unique and wonderful.

Maybe you get an unexpected bonus, a better-paid job or just some amazing luck. You taste success for a week or two, living life on a high, but then you soon drift back into normality - running out of money, before you run out month; wishing things were better, postponing that early retirement idea for another couple of years.

Whatever happens in this emotional cycle of boom and bust, you often fantasise about what it would be like to rich and successful. You hope, with the typical false hope that all losers love, that it will all get better soon. It is time for you to wake up and smell the coffee. Your life will NOT get any better unless you do something about it.

Unless you do something radical, things will not change. Insanity is defined as doing the same thing over and over again expecting a different result each time. Do not be insane, do not get mad about it, get tough about it.

Do not fall into the trap of hopelessness and failure. Do what you can to be successful. Look around. Lots of other bastards seem to be making it. Why shouldn't you? You know the kind of people I mean. People who are successful, but they are egotistical, tough and uncompromising. You do not really hate them, on the contrary you find them curiously likeable, but they are difficult to deal with if you get on their wrong side.

I know what it takes to be successful. I wrote this book to help victims like you. This book will change your mind about what you have to do to be more successful. It will have you laughing all the way to the bank at both the absurdity and simplicity of how it is done – how you can do it yourself.

"First secure an independent income, then practise virtue."
Greek proverb

In Britain and the United States a 'bastard' means someone whose is dislikeable, someone to be treated with contempt. In Australia, the word 'bastard' is a term of endearment - "You bastard," means, "Well done."

In this book, I use the words 'successful bastard' to mean something in between. Someone you have a sneaking admiration for, someone whose success you envy, but someone who is a bastard all the same.

Successful bastards are the 'lucky' few who have mastered being a total bastard at the exact moments when it will improve their position, but who operate with grace, good humour and intellect despite this. They manage to remain curiously likeable and interesting, developing great loyalty in their chosen circle, despite their dislikeable behaviour. They have an ability to turn the bastard in themselves off and on at will, just when it suits them. This builds into the successful way of life that this book will lead you to.

Successful bastards:

(1) Are independently wealthy

(2) Get what they want

(3) Do what they want.

$ecret Habit$ of $ucce$$ful Ba$tard$

All successful bastards have all three of these characteristics, and focus on developing them in that order. There is not much point doing what you want, if you never get what you want, nor doing either if you have no money to fund the fun and to fall back on when you want to do nothing. You need money to get what you want and to be able to do what you want.

The three characteristics, tie directly to wealth, power and happiness and you probably think that happiness is the most important. However, would you like to be happy and rich or happy and poor? Come to think of it, I would prefer to be *miserable* and rich than *miserable* and poor. Nothing makes being poor easy. If you find happiness in struggle, God bless you, but it is not for me.

When you are wealthy, many aspects of your happiness can be enhanced, from the provision of your basic needs through to enhancing your life by having thrilling new experiences. When you are poor, you struggle even to fulfil your basic needs, let alone have anything new to bring sparkle to your existence.

If someone tells you money cannot buy you love, just look at the next rich person's partner you see and ask yourself whether they would be with them if they were a poor, abject failure. Wealth gives no guarantee of happiness, but it certainly helps.

Similarly, if someone tells you that money cannot buy you health, that is true, but it can certainly help a lot. When you have the options of a personal trainer, ten holidays a year, a low stress lifestyle, regular private health screenings, daily massages and the very best nutrition that money can buy, it helps. Add copious leisure time to keep yourself fit the honest way, and you are improving your chances. In the future, good health will be the preserve of the wealthy and the lucky few. I do not intend to take the risk of hoping I am lucky with my health and neither should you.

There is a wonderful cycle that successful bastards get into. They generate personal wealth, which increases their power and influence, which in turn further increases their wealth. Their happiness is dependent on this cycle being maintained.

If you have lots of money, you have greater opportunities to invest and grow this wealth. It is a million times more difficult to turn £100 into £10M, than it is to turn £10M into £20M. If you had put £10M into randomly selected residential property ten years ago, it would now be worth £20M. £10 M profits, sitting in the bank, thank you very much. If you had invested £100, you would today be the proud owner of a very small worn-out shed.

Wealth is the key to starting the cycle. Power and happiness are the wonderful by-products.

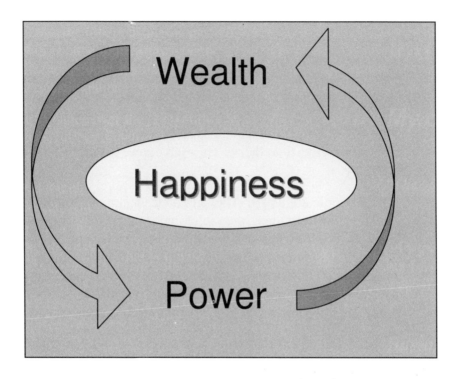

So how do some people make so much money, so much more than others? All wealthy people became that way because they are one of the following types. They are either:

(1) Uniquely talented,

(2) Lucky, or

(3) Self-made.

$ecret Habit$ of $ucce$$ful Ba$tard$

If they are uniquely talented, physically or intellectually, then they get paid a lot for doing something that comes naturally. They might be the schoolboy professional sportsman, the gifted singing prodigy, the stunning catwalk model or the financial whiz-kid. People pay them fortunes for what they have to give using only their natural resources and time. In many cases what they do comes easy to them. They have raw, unique talent you might say.

Other people are lucky. They get their wealth because someone gave it to them, they inherited it when someone died, they won it or they found it. A British newspaper, the Sunday Times, publishes a Rich List annually and it is interesting to note that in 1989 when the first Rich List was launched, 75 per cent of the people in it had inherited their wealth, but in 2007 the fortunes of 78 per cent of the people in it was self-made.

Even if you inherit a fortune, your success is not guaranteed. Look at the unfortunate Jamie Blandford, heir to the fabulous wealth of the dukedom of Marlborough, whose love affair with pharmaceuticals and alcohol led his father to disown him, caused him to spend a month in prison for forging prescriptions, a further six months in the slammer and suffer a three and a half year driving ban for dangerous driving and criminal damage following a road-rage incident. You still need to be smart to actually get that inheritance and then subsequently hang onto it.

The odds are against you having a unique talent or being lucky, so you are unlikely to make money this way. If you do, you will probably blow it and 'do a Jamie B' anyway. Which leaves you only one sure way to get rich - you have just got to be self-made.

This book explains how you can become a self-made success. It shows you how to exploit your limited potential, talents and resources to be successful. It pitches you into the competitive maelstrom of the masses of people who are also trying to do the very same thing. Only a few succeed. Only a few can wear the badge of the 'successful bastard' with the pride it deserves.

This book contains loads of useful information that will help you to become just as much of a bastard as you need to become to be successful. It will explain my own four stages of the successful bastard maturity model, taking you from novice through to expert status. You will understand the bastard's code of easy money making, as well as the philosophy and basic rules for living the life of a successful bastard.

You will learn the four secret habits of successful bastards, know 20 ways to be more of a bastard and have 100 techniques at your disposal to make sure your own transition happens comfortably and easily. You will have lots of quotations and anecdotal evidence from famous people to help you understand and remember the essential pieces of the process.

You will laugh throughout at the absurdity of what you learn and be amazed and shocked at how often the underlying messages make perfect sense. In short you will know how successful bastards operate and be able to change your behaviour to become one yourself whilst disabling anyone else playing nasty games with your life.

$ecret Habit$ of $ucce$$ful Ba$tard$

You will have a lot of fun measuring others using the bastard's bingo game. Ultimately, you will be able to measure exactly how much of a bastard you, or other people, are using the unique Bastardometer self-test questionnaire.

This book gives you that extra chance over the competition by telling you the secrets that successful bastards use to get wealthy, powerful and happy.

That being said, you will need to behave in ways that today might seem alien to you. However, you want success and I will show you how.

My only words of caution are: Be careful what you wish for.

"I believe in the Golden Rule, - the man with the gold, rules." Mr T.

Introduction

My objectives for writing this book

"The point is that you cannot be too greedy." Donald Trump

I would like to say that I wrote this book to improve humanity, but I would be lying to you and now is not the time to do that. I want you to know that I wrote this book to apply the....

Bastards' Code of Easy Money-Making:

(1) **Create something simple that people want**

(2) **Get others to help in ways that return more than you have to pay them**

(3) **Get lots of people to buy it, for more than it cost you to make it**

(4) **Expand into associated profitable business areas.**

$ecret Habit$ of $ucce$$ful Ba$tard$

Whatever Successful Bastards do they will use some form of this code to make their money. Whether you entertain, advise, manufacture, retail or invest, the trick is to create something saleable, sell it and profit from it many times over, but deliver what people see as value for the price paid.

I learned the value of this model in the software industry, where we would sell a few CD's and a few boxes of well written technical books and user guides to big companies for millions of dollars.

I am delighted to tell you that writing and publishing this book follows the Bastards' Code of Easy Money-Making perfectly:

(1)   Write a self-help book for the masses of nice but unsuccessful people

(2)   Get a friend to illustrate it and a cheap Chinese print shop to print it

(3)   Use the Internet to promote it and add a healthy mark-up on costs of production to arrive at a retail price

(4)   Build an interactive web-site, board game and fun-product line that people can spend more money on.

Benefits to you the reader

"In almost every act of our lives whether in the sphere of politics or business in our social conduct or our ethical thinking, we are dominated by the relatively small number of persons who understand the mental processes and social patterns of the masses. It is they who pull the wires that control the public mind." Edward L. Bernays

This book will be fun to read. I want you to laugh and enjoy the material - it is a funny subject. However, there is a serious side that I know will get you thinking differently about success.

Sometimes, the world around us seems overrun by 'successful bastards' and you wish you were a bit more of a bastard yourself. Deep down you want to be more like them do you not? You wish you had those qualities.

There is a little bit of the bastard in all of us, but most of us are not real bastards. We find it uncomfortable to go the whole hog and we spend our lives being outdone by others.

In the process of reading this book your eyes will be opened. If you take it a little seriously, and your eyes are wide open, it will make you more successful, happy and rich. I guarantee it.

However, I will not give you your money back if it does not work, because it will not have been my fault. You will not have tried hard enough. 'Self-made' means just that. It is up to you.

$ecret Habit$ of $ucce$$ful Ba$tard$

This book tells you what successful bastards really do to stay on top. It will give you an edge over the competition. When your eyes are fully opened you will be able to:

(1)   **Be more aware of how your behaviour affects your chances of success**

(2)   **Adopt some or all of their 'tricks' to make you more successful**

(3)   **Measure just how much of a bastard you and people around you are**

(4)   **Spot the bastards around you and counter-attack when they are working against you.**

You can learn how to be more of a bastard by reading this book and with the help of examples you can practise and perfect your skills as you do. It is not difficult and once you become focused on being more of a bastard and begin ignoring the suffering of others, you will be instantly more 'lucky', successful, powerful and wealthy.

I know this book will appeal to you, that part of you is in it, and you will gain a lot from reading it.

$ecret Habit$ of $ucce$$ful Ba$tard$

The unpalatable truth

"Truth would quickly cease to become stranger than fiction, once we got as used to it."   *Henry Louis Mencken*

This book is titled 'Secret Habits of Successful Bastards' for good reasons:

All successful self-made, uniquely gifted or just plain lucky people are one sort of bastard or another, at some time in their lives, they have to be

To make it, hold onto it and above all enjoy it, successful people have to be self-centred, tough, ruthless and unpredictable

Successful people do not share how they operate with ordinary people, so what they know is usually kept secret from the rest of us. Until now that is.

When you read any self-help book titled, 'How to Become a Billionaire', or whatever, there is one fundamental problem with what you read. The author is unlikely to tell you just how much of a bastard the people referenced had to be to succeed in the first place and then to stay there afterwards.

$ecret Habit$ of $ucce$$ful Ba$tard$

If the author is the successful person, then you can imagine why they would not tell you unpalatable things about how they made themselves successful. If they reference other people, that they have interviewed, then the same applies to what those people told the author.

There is also the problem of falling foul of libel laws, so authors are unlikely to say potentially damaging things about litigious billionaires that they have interviewed, even if they know the truth. Rich people worry about their reputation and they worry about getting found out and losing their status, wealth and position.

The best place you can get truthful data about how people made their fortunes is first hand. Even then, the successful bastard will not tell you everything.

You could do some research. You could read monolithic, unauthorised biographies of individuals and ferret out the juicy bits, but there is not time to read all those. Most well-connected and powerful people will not allow anything bad to be written about them in the first place. They will get an injunction to block publication beforehand, so many of the most truthful books never reach the public eye. Chances are then that you will not get to read everything you need to know. Some stuff is really, very secret.

As part of the research for this book I wrote to billionaires, captains of industry, heads of state, famous entertainers and people in the public eye. Many were generous in their replies, but most delegated the responses to their staff. This resulted in some outstanding replies including being wished the best of luck

$ecret Habit$ of $ucce$$ful Ba$tard$

with my book by HRH Prince Charles because his assistant failed to read what the subject matter was.

However, such generosity was not always shown. Most people simply apologised for not being able to participate because of "work commitments and scheduling constraints," thank you Larry Ellison, or with one liners like, "I don't believe you have to be a shit to succeed," thank you Sir John Harvey-Jones.

One billionaire who made his fortune in motor racing had his lawyer immediately send me a letter threatening me with legal action if I mentioned his name or used any part of the letter that was sent to me in this book. He was not wasting any time going on the offensive to stop me telling you what a selfish, tough and ruthless man he is.

Read the biography of any of the rich and famous and instead of the truth, the book will tell you all about the successful person's vision, planning, lifetime of hard work, leadership skills, financial brilliance, and so on. It will tell you about how to win people over, develop brilliant relationships with everyone, develop and market new creative ideas, and about how persistence and dedication won through, etc., etc., ad nausea.

The author will leave out loads of unpalatable and painful truths about how they really made it. They will give major credit to pleasant behaviours that were rarely seen in real-life and de-emphasise the impact or frequency of use of ones that would obviously appear distasteful to others.

$ecret Habit$ of $ucce$$ful Ba$tard$

They certainly will not tell you about any of their outrageous behaviours, their ruthlessly competitive and aggressive lifestyle, or that above all they think they are the most important person in the world. They will kid you on that they are friendly, compassionate and likeable, when everyone that knows them thinks they are vain, nasty, unforgiving and unreliable. Let us face it why would they tell anyone – not least Joe Public, their family, their employees or their shareholders - that they were total and utter bastards to deal with?

This book is different. It acknowledges that some of the most distasteful behaviours are pre-requisites for a successful lifestyle. You may disagree now, but I will bet you change your mind soon.

Lucky Bastards

"Luck is when opportunity knocks and you answer." **Anon**

There is no such thing as luck, just certain behaviours that expose a person to opportunity. If you want more luck, open your eyes and be more of a bastard more often.

Since there is no such thing as luck, there is no such thing as a lucky bastard. However, there are bastards for sure. We just assume that all the successful ones must be lucky. They are not. They work hard at being bastards and what looks like luck follows them around.

If you do not believe me, just read Richard Wiseman's book, 'The Luck Factor.' Richard is a psychologist and has been researching what makes people lucky for fifteen years. His conclusion is that people we might call 'lucky bastards' make luck happen through their attitude and behaviour. Attitudes and behaviours you will discover in the habits, traits, tips and techniques within this book.

Once you have the vision to spot opportunity, to make your own luck, you will have to be committed to making that thing happen positively in your favour, at all costs. Others will be looking to exploit the same opportunity and it is the biggest bastard that will keep hold of it and benefit from it.

$ecret Habit$ of $ucce$$ful Ba$tard$

All successful people are one sort of bastard or another. They are dedicated only to themselves, they are direct and forceful, painfully ruthless and you could not trust them if the chips were down. Their success is their only priority. Everything and everyone else in their way are dispensable when it suits them. They are successful bastards, plain and simple.

Now I know what you are thinking. "He is wrong. You can be nice and be successful." You are wrong. It cannot happen.

Stay being nice and you will not be as successful as you could be. If you still do not believe me, I will prove it to you. Read on.

The Quick Bastard Test

"You never get a second chance to make a first impression"
Anon

Try the quick bastard test.

Name three, rich, successful people you know personally and work out from what you know of them how much of a bastard they are. Which of the following character traits get ticked as applying to them?

If you do not know three rich, successful people, you need this book more than you thought. Skip the next bit and just get on with reading the book and practising being a bastard more often.

The Quick Bastard Test

	Person #1	Person #2	Person #3
They love themselves			
They are tough to deal with			
They never give up			
You cannot second guess them			
Total score			

28

$ecret Habit$ of $ucce$$ful Ba$tard$

I bet all three of the people you selected score at least three ticks out of a possible four.

Pause for a moment and consider what this means. The first three successful people you could think of are bastards. Here is a shocking bit of news for you. All successful people are bastards. Very successful people are egotistical, tough, tenacious and unpredictable bastards.

You cannot be rich, powerful and successful if you are kind, friendly, thoughtful and predictable. It just will not happen. Do not believe for one moment that you can be nice *and* successful. You cannot. There are too many sharks out there and they will eat you alive if you show any signs of weakness.

To make a lot of money, which is the founding root of personal success, you must exploit others. To survive you must make great efforts to protect yourself from those you exploit and from other bastards wishing to take what you have or copy what you have done.

There is not one business empire in the world or one family dynasty that has not based its wealth creation on the exploitation of others. In many cases criminal activities will have taken place to secure the foothold. It may only be tax avoidance, bribery, jettisoning partners without recourse, sacking people, threatening competitors or knowingly selling something which is dangerous, sub-standard or just plain bad value for money.

Those things are bad for sure, but they pale into insignificance when you think of the blackmail, extortion, kidnap, slavery, torture and murder that helped build many of the respectable family businesses and global corporations we know today. If

$ecret Habit$ of $ucce$$ful Ba$tard$

you think I am exaggerating, read on.

Many of the most famous captains of industry who are revered as role models for business leaders were evil, manipulative bastards and I will tell you who they are and what they did. Who would have thought for instance that the Astor family, once the richest in the world, would have part-founded their wealth on the back of smuggling narcotics around the world

To make money, you must exploit others and be prepared to operate in the shadowy world of deceit and corruption that is the world of business.

Having said that, you are probably now thinking, "OK, maybe this guy has a point. But there are other ways of making money where you do not exploit people." That is true, but only in part.

There are ways of making money without being a bastard and exploiting loads of people. However, they are few and far between. The only ways possible are that someone could give it to you, you could inherit it, you could win it or you could find it. Even then, you cannot benefit from these things happening to you without having been at least a bit of a bastard somewhere along the line.

If someone gives you lots of money the chances are that you have beaten everyone into submission that they might have given it to instead. Why else would they give it to you? Maybe you are a wealthy person's mistress or toy-boy. You can bet it was not a co-incidence that they gave *you* loads of money and that it did not come as a total surprise when it happened. Plus, I guarantee that someone more deserving lost out in the process.

$ecret Habit$ of $ucce$$ful Ba$tard$

If you inherit wealth, that is not good luck. Someone has died and you have been remembered either because of genetics or close association. Even if you have a blood relationship you still need to be calculatingly close so as not to get 'cut-out' of the will. If you were not related to the dead person, do not tell me you were friendly to them purely because you liked them and that money never entered your head, because that is just not true is it? You expected to get the money.

If you win it - you have gambled. It was no accident. Say you win £5M in the National Lottery. You have just taken a pound or two from millions of poor people who were clinging to the false hope that they could be rich. In effect, you shafted them.

If you find it, you must have been looking. Maybe it is that dusty old painting in the attic, that article in a charity shop, a bundle of notes in a holdall or buried treasure in your back garden. Sure as not, it was a conscious effort on your part to look for it or that having found it you spent a lot of effort getting it secretly valued and turned into money you can use. Once you realised its value you did not share it with anyone. You kept it all for yourself.

You might now be saying, "OK, maybe you do have to be a bastard to be successful, but that is a price I am not willing to pay," or, "I am too nice to be a bastard." Wake up friend. Life is a competitive challenge, not a leisurely break. You get what you deserve. If you want to help others, make a load of money now and you can be as nice as you like when you are older and independently secure.

$ecret Habit$ of $ucce$$ful Ba$tard$

➢ All successful people are one sort of bastard or another

➢ If you want more luck, be more of a bastard more often

➢ The biggest bastard will keep hold of the biggest opportunity

➢ Wealth is always created by the exploitation of others

➢ Make a load of money now and you can be as nice as you like when you are older and financially independent.

How to use this book

"The few who do are the envy of the many who only watch."
Jim Rohn

Getting what you want from this book

This book is crammed with useful hints, tips, techniques and examples organised in such a way that you can either read it front-to-back or just dip in and out as you see fit.

The margins throughout are nice and big for annotation to help you note who displays the characteristics as you go or to note something that you could improve upon, for better or worse.

If you are eager to get your 'Masters' in the subject matter, then make notes, observe, practise and revise. If you are not that committed just read it at your leisure.

Whoever you are, you will either be content with your life or unfulfilled. I would wager the latter, most people are – and that is good. This book will make you more fulfilled, confident in yourself and happier in life.

$ecret Habit$ of $ucce$$ful Ba$tard$

If you are content, that is fine as well. You will probably be doing most of the things I recommend already and as you read you can smugly pat yourself on the back, self-assured that you have it all under control.

There is an art to becoming a successful bastard, but it is not a 'black art'. It is true that no-one ever openly teaches you how to be a bastard, so to some extent it is a mystery, but in the main it is easy once you know how. It simply involves knowing all the interpersonal techniques that you can use on others and how to apply them so that you get your own way.

Mastery depends on you knowing when to use the techniques and assessing how best to counter others who are working against you. You have a lifetime to practice, but you are a long time dead, so I suggest strongly that you start immediately.

The next chapters explain the four secret habits of successful bastards. Each chapter focuses on one habit and will explore five traits which collectively make the habit real.

Each trait has five supporting techniques that allow you to develop them fully. So for each habit, you will have 25 techniques to note, observe in others and practise yourself.

Each technique is explained in simple terms, with examples of real-life application and suggestions on how and when to best use them. I have used examples of some well-known people who have exhibited the habits, traits and techniques to show you that they work and how they have affected that person's success.

$ecret Habit$ of $ucce$$ful Ba$tard$

I have tried to make this book an easy read and to provide humorous anecdotes from real life to make the points and because humour sells books. After all, life is supposed to be fun. We are aiming to become successful bastards, not miserable bastards.

Successful bastards laugh a lot at the expense of others. I chuckle every time someone buys this book for example.

"You must always work not just within but below your means. If you can handle three elements, handle only two. If you can handle ten, then handle only five. In that way the ones you do handle, you handle with more ease, more mastery, and you create a feeling of strength in reserve."
Pablo Picasso

Successful Bastards' Bingo

"When you do the common things in life in an uncommon way, you will command the attention of the world." George Washington Carver

I have developed an on-line game on my web-site that you can play to hone your skills at spotting how successful bastards' behaviour works. You can use this simple and fun exercise to brighten up dull meetings, family gatherings or even when you are alone to see how well you, or someone else, behaved like a bastard at some point in time.

Pick the biggest bastard you know, watch them and listen carefully, marking off the 'numbers' Bingo-style when they exhibit the trait marked. Try starting with your boss at one of those meetings where poor business performance figures are being discussed.

When you make a line, four corners or - if they are really going to town - a full house, shout, "Bingo!" With luck only a select few will know what you have been doing and be able enjoy the moment with you.

Try Bastards' Bingo yourself at the web-site below.

Measuring your score on the Bastardometer

"The only man who behaved sensibly was my tailor; he took my measurement anew every time he saw me, while all the rest went on with their old measurements and expected them to fit me." George Bernard Shaw

The questionnaire behind the Bastardometer allows you to measure how much of a bastard someone is by recording how often they exhibit particularly dislikeable, but powerfully persuasive, traits. At its basic level it allows you to score yourself or others on how much of a bastard you/they are. Over time you can plot your improvement.

The Bastardometer is a scoring scale, embedded behind the questionnaire, which allows you to accurately and consistently measure how people's behaviour ranks in terms of its level of power over other people. Marking how often a person exhibits each of 100 dislikeable traits, the Bastardometer will automatically calculate their position on the scale, translating this into a percentage score, giving a phrase to describe them and providing a narrative summary of the person being measured.

Each person will be classified as being between a 'Saintly Failure' and a 'Total and Utter Successful Bastard' depending on how highly they score.

The Bastardometer has a built in set of weightings, giving greater emphasis to some of your chosen traits than others. For example, *stealing things* is more offensively powerful than *getting more than you need* all the time, so it carries more weight as a result.

You can go online to my web-site shown at the bottom of the page and interactively measure yourself and others. You can request a classy printed certificate be produced to recognise your status formally.

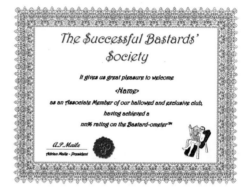

If you are dealing with a particularly nasty bastard you might like to give them their certificate as a present to let them know that you are on to them.

"Until a man is twenty-five, he still thinks, every so often, that under the right circumstances he could be the baddest motherfucker in the world. If I moved to a martial-arts monastery in China and studied real hard for ten years. If my family was wiped out by Colombian drug dealers and I swore myself to revenge. If I got a fatal disease, had one year to live, and devoted it to wiping out street crime. If I just dropped out and devoted my life to being bad." Neal Stephenson

Mastering being a successful bastard

"I would like to live like a poor man with lots of money."
Pablo Picasso

Basic philosophy

Life is a game; play to win, play hard, take no prisoners and have fun.

The first step in basic training is to make a decision to change how you judge things around you. You have to learn to see the world differently.

Think of life as a gloriously complex and advanced game. You are a player and almost everybody else on the planet is playing against you. Life is supposed to be highly competitive. Ask Charles Darwin.

$ecret Habit$ of $ucce$$ful Ba$tard$

Your competition will fall into one of five groups of people:

Wimps	lightweight, boring, failures
Whingers	miserable, depressed saboteurs
Wasters	time-wasting, high-maintenance nuisances
Wankers	jumped-up, pompous idiots
Winners	self-centred, tough, ruthless risk takers.

The first four groups are the targets of your contempt. Think of them as your enemies. They will at best slow you down; at worst they will actively compete against you. Be a bastard to all of them. They will do nothing for you, so be brutal.

Only the *winners* get your respect. They are the people with whom you will operate as near equals, with whom you will plan and build your success.

There will not be many winners, so choose them carefully. Know who they are soon. Some will be found in your immediate family, close friends or trusted lieutenants, but most are out there for you to find in new acquaintances.

$ecret Habit$ of $ucce$$ful Ba$tard$

If you are really fortunate, your close associates are already all winners. If not, you would better get to work on the ones that are not immediately. You must not carry any passengers on this journey. Think only of your own best interests, be tough with people that will not add value to your cause, ruthlessly pursue your ambitions and keep people guessing what your next step will be.

"There are two ways not to suffer from the inferno we are all living in every day. The first suits most people: accept the inferno and become part of it to the point where you don't even see it any more. The second is riskier and requires constant attention and willingness to learn: seek out and know how to recognize whoever and whatever, in the midst of the inferno, is not inferno, and help them last, give them space."

Italo Calvino

Rules of the game successful bastards play

"Step outside the guidelines of the official umpires and make your own rules and your own reality." Phil Ochs

The game successful bastards play has one unique characteristic. They make the rules.

This game is fantastic fun and you can win prizes of unbelievable value if you win. Successful bastards play the game whether you take part or not. It does not stop when you decide not to play.

It carries on, 24 hours a day, every day of the year. The players that have the confidence to keep playing will be the winners. If you are not one of them, you lose.

If you play the game well, the rewards far outweigh the risks, but you have to be brave to play the game and be prepared to play it for real. There are too many competitors after the prizes for you to be complacent.

To win you must spot and seize opportunities that will improve your life. Believe in yourself and be tough. Once you decide to do something, let no-one stand in your way. Trust no-one and encourage no-one to trust you. Make your own rules. Here are two golden rules of mine.

1.   Never tell anyone everything

2.

As I said, make your own rules. Write yours down as you go, you will find plenty of inspiration within this book. The habits, traits, tips and techniques you will discover will inspire you to establish your unique rules as you play the game life.

When you have written out your favourites, pin them up somewhere where you will read them every day. I would recommend inside your wardrobe, on the back of your bedroom door or on the wall in your home and workplace.

How to make your own luck

"I believe in luck; how else can you explain the success of those you dislike?" Jean Cocteau

I like to think you are lucky you picked this book up. You are probably not a bastard. At least not yet, you are not. However, read this book and practise diligently and you are well on the way to changing your life by becoming a very successful bastard.

I hope this book will take pride of place in your home and that you will reference it regularly. For this reason, I recommend you leave a copy in your toilet - ideally on a shelf to be read whilst you are otherwise engaged, rather than in the toilet itself.

The playwright, Tom Stoppard, once wrote:

"All your life you live so close to the truth, it becomes a permanent blur in the corner of your eye, and when something nudges it into outline it is like being ambushed by the grotesque."

$ecret Habit$ of $ucce$$ful Ba$tard$

I am going further than 'nudging it into outline' in this book, more like 'making it blindingly clear,' so the contents may well appear utterly grotesque to you the reader. If they do, I do not apologise. Far from it - it is time your eyes were opened.

I think the whole subject of becoming more successful by being more a bastard is hilarious. I am astounded daily at how self-centred, nasty, evil and inconsiderate people maintain positions of great power and how the most successful people use techniques like those in this book all the time to improve their position, beat off opponents and get their own way.

There are a few natural bastards out there for sure. Truly evil sociopaths and psychopaths, but no-one likes them and they will get their come-uppance because of it eventually.

The people I find amusing and intriguing are the ones that calculate what they do specifically so to get the best advantage for themselves. They operate consciously and they adopt the behaviour of bastards when required, to suit themselves.

Meet successful bastards at any social engagement and they are great fun to be with. They are clearly self-serving and dominate the proceedings, but everyone loves them for that.

They are not natural bastards; they just turn in on when required. These individuals are something we should all aspire to be. They are successful bastards.

It is OK to be a successful bastard

"I believe in giving everything my best shot. I do not believe in holding back. I am very driven by the fact that we are destined with these opportunities."
Shailendra Singh

Successful bastards have everything you want. They have the cars, the houses, the gorgeous spouse, the sex, the friends, the material goods, all the money and all the fun. They represent everything you could have been if only you had had a bit more luck. At least that is what you think.

It is OK to be a bastard and be successful. In fact it is the only way to get there if you are an average person. 'Successful bastard' means something different than just a bastard. The word 'bastard' transforms into a good word when used with the word 'successful'. It no longer means someone to be treated with contempt. It means someone you, and others, aspire to become.

Everyone deep down wants to be a successful bastard and there is a very good chance you will be one soon. I hope you enjoy the experience.

$ecret Habit$ of $ucce$$ful Ba$tard$

All you need to know about being a successful bastard

"The best time to plant a tree is 20 years ago. The second best time is now." Anon

This book will tell you all you need to know about being a successful bastard and you can measure your progress as you go.

This book explores the world in which successful bastards live. You will discover four secret habits of successful bastards. You will discover techniques that the world's greatest bastards have used to become rich, powerful and successful.

You will discover how to make the four habits uniquely yours. For each habit, you will explore five traits, each mastered by applying five simple techniques. In all, you will have 100 techniques to draw upon to help you to become a successful bastard.

The whole process will amuse you. Many of the techniques can be applied with humour and I know when you become aware of them and spot other people using them you will find it funny.

I have even included an easy-to-play 'Bastard's Bingo' game that you can play with loved ones, friends, colleagues and bosses.

At any stage you will be able to measure how much of a successful bastard you are with the aid of an automated self-test that will tell you clearly how you have progressed on what I call the Bastardometer. You can also score other people or get them to score you.

My favourite exercise is for couples to score each other and compare the results to their view of themselves. It is a guaranteed eye-opener and will provoke lots of discussion. You are more of a bastard than you think you are.

Being a bastard is simple. There are just four habits you must exhibit to be successful. They were secret until now. You need simply to be:

Self-centred

Tough

Ruthless, and

Unpredictable

Do it

Today

and *STRUT* your stuff.

The Four Levels of Self-Satisfaction

"One of the symptoms of an approaching nervous breakdown is the belief that one's work is terribly important." **Bertrand Russell**

I worked diligently for five years after leaving school before I realised you were allowed to be your own person and do your own thing.

For me, work was just an extension of school, being separated as it was by just six short days. I had started work urgently, having got married whilst still at school; I needed money for the imminent birth of our first daughter, a place to live and food for the family.

I did what I was told and never overstepped the mark. I treated my supervisors like my parents, with the greatest respect possible. I never argued, spoke out, swore or behaved in a difficult manner. I took what was sent my way without complaint. I was fortunate to be sharp and this allowed me to survive. However, I was not flourishing. I was doing what I was told, no more, no less. I was at what I call **Level Zero - Obedience**.

By 23 years of age it dawned on me that this was not doing me much good. Doing what you are told is unsatisfying and soul destroying. Do what YOU want instead. It really worked well

$ecret Habit$ of $ucce$$ful Ba$tard$

for me when I started doing what I wanted, not what I was told.

I soon became the fastest promoted and highest paid person in the company. I hassled and quizzed my managers, competed with my colleagues and fought for the best jobs internally. It was easy and a lot more fun than doing what I was told. I call this stage **Level One - Awareness**.

At Level One, I used to be a bit of a bastard, but I still used to work hard and long hours for an ungrateful employer and I used to care about most of the people I worked with. I earned a considerable amount of money for what I did, but never quite shook off the overdraft. Then one day it hit me.

I realised that success, and by that I mainly mean cash, goes to people who want it above all else. They want it for themselves and they have no qualms about taking advantage of others to get it.

I changed my approach and became more successful in the process. I moved to **Level Two - Exploitation**. I became more self-centred, tough and ruthless than ever before.

The top guys seemed to me to be unpredictable, so I added this to my repertoire. I added a level of unreliability that fitted my status in the companies I worked for. I operated like this for another 15 years, making loads of money, until I realised that an even more advanced way of being successful existed. **Level Three was born - Achievement**.

At Level Three, I finally took the plunge and stopped working for others. I chose my projects and I started several companies and decided to write a book about how people really become

$ecret Habit$ of $ucce$$ful Ba$tard$

successful.

 I did not rush this book because my golf handicap needed some serious reduction and I had a lot of pleasurable hobbies to pursue. I became totally self-centred and focused on my own success and that is exactly what I got in return

OBEDIENCE	LEVEL 0	DO AS YOU ARE TOLD
AWARENESS	LEVEL 1	WORK HARD DOING WHAT *YOU* WANT
EXPLOITATION	LEVEL 2	TAKE ADVANTAGE OF OTHERS
ACHIEVEMENT	LEVEL 3	FOCUS ONLY ON YOUR SUCCESS

The types of people that make successful bastards

"I believe that one becomes stronger emotionally by taking life less personally. If your employer criticises your report, do not take it personally. Instead, find out what is needed and fix it. If your girlfriend laughs at your tie, do not take it personally. Find another tie or find another girlfriend." Marilyn vos Savant

If you have ever wondered why you have failed to reach your full potential, I can tell you why. You are too nice. You are too soft. You care too much about people and not enough about yourself.

"But no," I hear you say, "I know so-and-so and they are really nice and they are successful." You are wrong. You do not know them well enough. Think about them again......
The world of successful bastards is inhabited by people of every age, race, creed and background. They are not selective about who joins their ranks. No one reviews applications.

> ➢ **Forget about being nice to people; stop being soft**

> ➢ **Becoming a successful bastard is your decision.**

$ecret Habit$ of $ucce$$ful Ba$tard$

Why bastards are successful

"If we do not succeed, we run the risk of failure." George W. Bush Jnr

For most people, success is measured in terms of disposable income and quality of life. Quality of life is about having the time to do what you want with the people you want to be with. Money and 'free-time' are the key metrics. You need lots of money to do what you really want to do and lots of time to do it in.

If you are jealous and envious and cannot understand how successful bastards achieved their success when you have not, remind yourself that they MADE it happen through their effort, attitude and behaviour.

In truth, it is all down to them being focused on themselves, overbearing on others, ruthless with everyone and reckless to the point of madness. If you do not believe me, read on.

➢ **Spend more time with your money**

➢ **Make things happen by being more of a bastard.**

$ecret Habit$ of $ucce$$ful Ba$tard$

Why being nice gets you nowhere

"You can get more with a kind word and a gun than you can with a kind word alone." Al Capone

Do you think successful people are amiable, friendly, gentle, pleasant people? Think of what you know and what you have heard about successful people. Imagine how difficult it must have been for them to get successful.

Imagine how hard it is to build a business empire or become a wealthy celebrity, or even just to maintain more than one large house, let alone to win through to the top in our highly competitive world. Imagine the hurdles they have jumped - the difficulties and failures they have had to overcome.

You can be sure that the people who have made it have been rascals to get there. They think only of themselves. They are often offensive, they are forceful and you could not trust them if the chips were down. Their success is their only priority. Everything and everyone in their way are dispensable when it suits them.

The successful person has no qualms about upsetting anyone - no matter whether they are spouses, kids, family, friends, acquaintances, colleagues, employees, bosses, partners, sub-ordinates, competitors or people in the street. They exploit people to satisfy themselves. They are bastards by any definition of the word. Remember though that being a bastard does not necessarily make you a bad person. On the contrary, lots of people will love and respect you for it.

- ➤ **To overcome difficulty and failure, you must be tough**
- ➤ **Think only of yourself**
- ➤ **Exploit others**
- ➤ **People will love and respect you if you are more of a bastard.**

$ecret Habit$ of $ucce$$ful Ba$tard$

You wish you were tougher and you can be

"When angry count to four, when very angry, swear." Mark Twain

Toughness is a state of mind. We all have the capacity and capability to be much, much stronger than we are, both mentally and physically. Most of us do not bother developing these skills.

Once you stop worrying about other people, you will find that being tough is easy. It is much easier than being kind, caring, empathetic, thoughtful and fair. It requires little mental effort and blocks out confusing and potentially distracting emotions. It is like being a martial artist, so daily practise is essential.

Be colder when you next approach a problem. Consequences are irrelevant until they adversely affect you, so do not waste time thinking about them unless they do.

If you are in any doubt, try thinking, "What would *'blank'* do in this situation?" substituting the name of the biggest bastard you know for *'blank'*. The answer will soon come to you.

$ecret Habit$ of $ucce$$ful Ba$tard$

➢ **You have the capacity and capability to be tougher**

➢ **Stop worrying about other people**

➢ **Be colder when problem solving**

➢ **Ask yourself, "What would _____ do in this situation?"**

Good reasons to be nice to people

How to develop the secret habits of successful bastards

"Life is not easy for any of us. But what of that? We must have perseverance and above all confidence in ourselves. We must believe that we are gifted for something and that this thing must be attained." Marie Curie

The secret habits of successful bastards support your ultimate goal; the achievement of success. Memorise the habits, internalise them and believe in them. Make a point of understanding the fundamentals. We will be examining the detail of each and exploring 25 techniques for making each happen in later chapters. As you go, make notes relevant to your situation and commit to making changes happen.

Before you read on, practise suspending judgment. When you read something that at first seems harsh, intense, impractical or downright painful to execute; pause.

Play-through the behaviour as if you were applying it for real somewhere. Massage the proposed behaviour around in your mind. Position whatever habit or technique is being explored in terms of your life experience. Imagine what would have happened if you had used more of that approach when dealing with a difficult situation that did not go your way in the past sometime.

Avoid the classic 'denial' response of putting your head in the sand. It will be challenging to do some of things I have suggested, but the benefits will be great. Stay out of denial and try to think through how such behaviours would be acceptably played out in your life, in your office, in your home. There is no black and white here. Just shades of grey.

You will have already carried off some of the behaviours like a master, others you will pick up immediately, whilst some will always seem uncomfortable and foreign to you. You should pick and mix those techniques that work for you and use them as 'tricks' when YOU think they will have a positive effect on your life. Many of the techniques may seem abhorrent, some you will refuse to accept as being worthwhile applying. No matter.

Whichever tens of techniques you apply from the 100 beneath the secret habits, you will possess an enviable 'success kitbag'. Even if you cannot apply some of them, you will see them when others use them against you and be more prepared to respond. Do not forget here that we are talking about you deciding when and how hard to apply these techniques. They are for you and your benefit.

You may think that being selfish, greedy and lazy will not get you very far on the success ladder for instance. Think again. For most of these techniques you can put the word 'selectively' in front of them and the meaning remains the same. There is little point in me putting this word in front of each technique since it applies to the majority.

I am not suggesting that you must ALWAYS behave in the prescribed way, but that it should be your start point in every situation. You must assess, using what you know about your own capability to execute and the need versus the opportunity in-hand, how far to go with the behaviour. A later chapter deals with how to avoid going too far, so for now you should look to your acceptable maximum levels of application.

You should do what you feel comfortable doing, because above all it is you who is going to do it and then live with the consequences. After a while you will get much better at feeling comfortable about being more of a bastard. I promise.

For example, being lazy is good for you when faced with doing something that will not improve your position at all. If it is cheaper to get someone to so something than do it yourself, then be lazy. If it is not worth doing, then do not do it at all. Measure your effort in terms of return and all of a sudden, loads of things you do every day are pointless. Stop doing them now, get 'selectively' lazy.

Similarly, with being selfish and greedy; why should you not be so? Do not spend more money than you need to, make sure you get the biggest slice of the cake, enjoy conspicuous consumption. What is wrong with that?

$ecret Habit$ of $ucce$$ful Ba$tard$

Have lots of possessions, eat in the finest restaurants and throw the most lavish parties. Enjoy life. You are supposed to. Living like this will bring a lot of colour into a lot of people's lives, especially yours.

In the same way that 'selectively' is an unnecessary prefix on every technique, so are prefixes like 'over-', 'super-' and 'ultra-'. They add little value if repeated in front of every technique. However, I encourage you to think of these extremes, because that is where you will have to play to be fully successful. Being confident for instance is great, but being super-confident will blow people away.

"Even if you haven't encountered great success yet, there is no reason you can't bluff a little and act like you have. Confidence is a magnet in the best sense of the word. It will draw people to you and make your daily life... and theirs... a lot more pleasant." Donald Trump

The four secret habits are very simple, but very powerful and they give you a solid foundation and reference point for when you are living the successful life. There will be moments when you will wonder what to do for the best. The habits give you that solid, memorable foundation on which to make a decision if you are in doubt. The more you practise and apply them, the more you will instantly make decisions that will be in your favour.

The secret habits combine to make you powerful and successful; and believe me, they work.

> **Memorise, internalise and build your belief in the habits and techniques**

> **Massage, position and imagine them working for you as you use them selectively**

> **Pick 'n' Mix the tricks into your own 'success kit-bag'**

> **Make 'tough' your start point, then over-, super- and ultra-emphasise as needed**

> **Practice makes perfect.**

The Four $ecret Habit$ of $ucce$$ful Ba$tard$

Habit #1 - Look after number one

"To love oneself is the beginning of a lifelong romance."
Oscar Wilde

Life is not a team sport. You play alone. You come into the world with nothing and leave the same way, so do not waste any time while you are here. Above all else, look after number one.

If you are successful so will your family be and so will your friends and colleagues be. However, if you fail to put yourself first, everyone around you will fall by the wayside.

Nobody ever remembers the name of the silver or bronze medal winner. How many CD music compilations have you seen on sale titled 'Greatest Number 2's of the 1980's'. The gap between first and second can be miniscule, but the difference is gigantic. Play to win every time.

In some cultures, particularly the British, people have a peculiar distaste for winners. This stems from the basic beliefs of 'justice' and 'fair play' that pervade the culture. The successful bastards amongst us know that this culture creates losers, not winners.

I am sure in your life they have been times when you have focused on what you want to do. You have been indulgent and

$ecret Habit$ of $ucce$$ful Ba$tard$

spoiled yourself. Have a think about some of those times now.........

If, like most people, you rarely indulge yourself, you will have struggled to remember the last time you did exactly what you wanted to do, but you will I am sure have remembered one or two occasions when you did. They were good weren't they? You felt good afterwards.

Successful bastards indulge themselves all the time. They feel good about themselves all the time. They put themselves first.

Remember the one you love is you. It is OK to love yourself. Everyone should. The beauty of being focused on number one is that you only need think about yourself. It is easy. It is a most wonderful way to be and you can do so all on your own-some, with no help from anyone else. Self-taught, self-driven, self-centred, successful bastards are the best kind.

Most people go through life thinking about other people and how their own actions impact on those around them. Successful bastards, on the other hand, never think about other people unless they can further their own interests by doing so. They think the world revolves around them. They take self-satisfaction to its limit.

The *Queen of Mean*, Anne Robinson the journalist and broadcaster and now world famous host of "The Weakest Link" TV quiz, describes the culture that her businesswoman mother bestowed upon on her from an early age as being, "Last in the queue, first on the bus."   Anne says that she had one ambition in life, "To be famous," and her self-centred attitude has delivered her just that.

$ecret Habit$ of $ucce$$ful Ba$tard$

The intriguing thing you will discover when you become more self-centred is that people will look up to you and admire you even though deep down most people would say that being so would make a person dislikeable. When someone describes a self-centred successful person they will use positive adjectives like, "a real character, clever, charismatic, fun to be with, super-confident, a born winner....." People will always highlight your positive characteristics and overlook the negative ones, so be confident and make sure your nest is fully feathered as quickly as possible.

If you have unfulfilled dreams - think of yourself more often. No-one will mind if you do. On the contrary, they fully expect you to. That is a universally accepted part of being successful.

➢ **Believe in yourself**

➢ **Play to win, no-one remembers who came second**

➢ **Put yourself first**

➢ **Indulge and spoil yourself**

➢ **Fulfil all your dreams.**

Habit #2 - Wield your power

"It is better to be feared than loved, if you cannot be both."
Niccolo Machiavelli

The game of life is highly demanding, aggressive and potentially dangerous. Other people will be trying to win and they will be competing against you. If you assume that they will stop at nothing to win, you had better retaliate before they attack. Assume that people will try and get one over on you at the first opportunity, so be prepared to use the pre-emptive strike by demanding the best and being tough enough to stay the course.

If you are cunning, your premature retaliatory gestures will keep people in check and make sure that they do not begin to consider attacking you. Sub-consciously they will think that if you are like this when they are not attacking you, God only knows how troublesome you will be if they do. They will not be able to pluck up the courage to initiate anything against your wishes.

If you wonder what is going on here, it is because you did not realise that attack is the best form of defence in many situations. As they say, every battle is won before it starts. Read Sun Tzu's, "The Art of War," to develop your strategies fully.

$ecret Habit$ of $ucce$$ful Ba$tard$

Getting your retaliation in first advances the battle faster than your opponents can keep up with. It creates engagement when others are not ready to compete, thereby weakening their position dramatically. It creates a platform for success moulded to what you want to happen, not what someone else does. It makes you appear a formidable opponent from the outset.

> **Attack is often the best form of defence**

> **Retaliate before they attack**

> **Master the pre-emptive strike**

> **Justice and fair play creates losers, not winners**

> **Be formidable.**

$ecret Habit$ of $ucce$$ful Ba$tard$

Habit #3 - Never give up

"We are not retreating – we are advancing in another direction." General Douglas Macarthur

Once you are committed to playing the game - failure is not an option. You must be ruthlessly unstoppable. Your aims and objectives must be met, every time. If you get everything done your way you will open up the beautiful world of satisfaction that successful bastards enjoy.

Shake off the fear culture of losers because winners take all. Make yourself a winner by making definite decisions and keeping focussed on achieving your aims. Never give up. Get what you want done and get it done your way.

Duncan Bannatyne, the famous British entrepreneur, went from being a Navy stoker to building a £115M fortune by doing things his way and never giving up. Bannatyne believes, "....you never need to pay for an expensive consultant," and in all his businesses from ice cream vans, old people's home and a hotel, to fitness clubs and casinos, he got things done his way by investing his own money and making key decisions based on his common-sense.

Bannatyne believes his success in building the businesses rest on his skilful delegation to his management team, but it is clear that his original businesses were first established because he was fearless, ruthless in pursuing his aims and he did whatever it took to be successful.

You too must be prepared to fight relentlessly and determinedly for what you want. You must also be prepared to punish anyone who stands in your way. Remember that you will have to be cruel to be kind to anyone who presents barriers to your success.

> **Shake off the fear culture**

> **Make firm decisions and stick to them**

> **Never surrender**

> **Punish failure**

> **Be cruel to those who stand in your way.**

Habit #4 - Keep everyone guessing

"The President has kept all of the promises that he intended to keep." - George Stephanopolous (aide to Bill Clinton)

On those rare occasions when someone has got one over on you, I bet you have mostly been surprised and felt let down. I bet you have been surprised that the person or organisation could do it to you and have been left reeling from the experience. If you knew it was coming, it came as less of a shock and when it did, you were able to deal with it more quickly, rationally and completely than if it had been unexpected.

Use the power of the dagger whilst hiding it under your cloak. Make sure that people cannot read you or predict your next actions. Be prepared to change tack when needed and to let people down on a whim. Think nothing of being duplicitous and dishonest. You have to be to compete with those around you. Take the sorts of risks that others would not dare to and live life on the edge.

You may think my prescription is would result in an unpleasant life, that it will be distasteful to be unfathomable and unreliable. On the contrary, it makes for a comfortable and predictable existence for you and that is all that matters.

$ecret Habit$ of $ucce$$ful Ba$tard$

Anything goes as far as you are concerned and people will get used to your eccentric and confusing behaviour. They know you will stop at nothing to achieve your aims and whilst everyone around you is trying to second-guess what you will do, you will be free to pursue whichever direction takes your fancy, no matter how risky it may appear.

- ➢ **Use your cloak and dagger**

- ➢ **Confuse people**

- ➢ **Create mystery**

- ➢ **Do whatever it takes**

- ➢ **Be prepared to risk everything.**

The Four $ecret Habit$ of $ucce$$ful Ba$tard$

#1	**Look after number one**
#2	**Wield your power**
#3	**Never give up**
#4	**Keep everyone guessing**

#1 Look after number one

Five ways to build your strength

"All supposedly 'selfless' acts are entirely selfish. When a man gives to charity, rest assured he values the happiness it brings him more than the money itself. If he did not, he would not give his money away." James Halloran

Love yourself, for there is nothing finer in life. If you do not love yourself, how can you expect anyone else to love you? You are a fantastic machine with potential beyond your wildest dreams so live up to that potential. Whilst you are at it - love your money, love material things, love being a consumer and love your leisure time. Love things that make the one you love the most feel good.

Looking after number one is all about you. It is about being focused on what you want, focused on yourself. There is nothing wrong with being self-centred. On the contrary, it is a pre-requisite for success. When the going gets tough, it is your self-centredness that will keep you on track.

$ecret Habit$ of $ucce$$ful Ba$tard$

Strong people are self-centred. Self-centred people are **confident, competitive, selfish, greedy and lazy**. By developing these traits you will have five ways to be more self-centred.

Think of these traits as positive qualities, even though to express them requires a splendid disregard for others. Take a moment to convince yourself that if you really do care about 'number one' then these are essential habits to develop.

Being highly confident is the start-point so you must be very confident at all times. Be super-confident. Think Captain Confidence. You have just as much right to be confident as the next person.

"But I am naturally shy," I hear you say, "I could never be confident." Sorry; but I disagree. Even very confident people will tell you in a private moment that really, deep down, they feel a bit shy and nervous at times, almost everyone does. Everyone except for super-confident individuals, that is. They never show signs of weakness even in private moments. They are something spectacular to behold.

Confident individuals will not accept they are at fault. They believe that they can achieve anything they set their minds upon. They are focused, painfully tenacious and doggedly determined. Deep down, they are no different than you are. They have just refused to appear to be weak. You should do the same.

$ecret Habit$ of $ucce$$ful Ba$tard$

Self-belief of this kind can be acquired. Instead of looking around and worrying about why you are not as successful as other people, believe that you can achieve and you will. You are unique and special. Be totally sure of yourself.

My wife, Hilary, is very confident about herself. She often walks around the house singing a little song to the tune of 'Glory, Glory, Alleluia' that she made up which goes like this:

"I am the greatest in the world, Oh I am the greatest in the world, I am the greatest in the world, Oh yes, oh yes, I am." When I read this paragraph to her as I was writing it, her first reaction was, "Oh no! Everyone's going to know I love myself." After a short pause to reconsider she said, "I can live with that," and walked away humming the tune to herself. She is a class act.

You need to think more like my wife does. You need to believe that you are the greatest person on the planet. I do not love my wife any the less because she thinks she is the greatest person in the world. On the contrary, I find it fascinating that she truly believes this and admire her courage and commitment, even if she might appear conceited because of it.

To help with your self-confidence always keep yourself physically fit and mentally alert. Dress as expensively as you can, wear an exclusive watch and one or two fine pieces of jewellery and always polish your shoes, it will make a massive difference to the way you feel. It is a little known fact that head waiters allocate the best tables to the man wearing the best watch and the newest looking heels on their shoes. Now you know the two distinguishing marks of success used by tip-hungry rascals, make sure you do not let yourself down next time you are eating out.

Once you have tackled being more confident about yourself, becoming a **competitive** force is pretty easy. Being deliberately competitive is life enhancing. You may not realise, but you already are very competitive. It is a basic, genetic and instinctive characteristic, passed down from those times when we had to compete with everything around us simply to survive. You do not need wildlife programmes or anthropology documentaries at one o'clock in the morning to remind you that you are naturally competitive. We all are and always have been.

We love winners, we love winning. Do not be shy. Recognise the competitiveness in you, harness it and make it work for you every day. Competitiveness breeds goal setting, drives extraordinary effort and creates a success culture, so bring competition into everything you do.

If you really want to succeed, compete where you know you will win and if it looks like you are losing, change the game, the rules or the players. You want to win at all costs and you want them to lose. Being highly competitive gives you a wonderfully self-centred streak, as does being selfish.

Some of the most wonderful people I know are also the most **selfish**. They are indulgent and spend most of the time worrying about how things will affect them and conspiring for the outcome to be in their favour.

$ecret Habit$ of $ucce$$ful Ba$tard$

The richest people I know in financial terms are also the most mean with their cash, they are the ones who will spend the minimum unless they are the main beneficiary. Common sense really. A fool and his (her) money are easily parted, as they say.

For example, is throwing lavish parties a selfish or generous action? It depends on your point of view. If you ask people who throw them why they do, they will tell you candidly that it is less about selflessness and more about improving their image, networking with important people and beefing up their inflated egos. To give an air of generosity to the proceedings, they will usually add that they like to 'give a little back'. Think what this means. They must have TAKEN something in the first place, to have to give it back. So much for generosity!

Lavish party-givers are careful about who to invite, with the guest list carefully screened for maximum personal advantage. It is great public relations and it often makes up for them being a total bastard for the rest of the year. This is why corporations throw lavish summer and Christmas parties for their downtrodden employees and disgruntled customers. Note too, that they only do this when the going is good and the fat cats are getting fatter. As soon as the purse strings tighten, entertainment is the first thing to be cut sharply back. You can bet your life that the party-giver also gets the best table, the best service, the entertainment they want, the finest booze and food, and unbounded adulation for being such a wonderful person. Giving a little back? Humbug!

I like people who over-consume, people who have everything. They are good to be around and great to know. They are **greedy**, for sure, but their abundant lifestyles are filled with excitement and stimulation and they drag people along in their wake. Develop a lust for consumption and materialism. Surround yourself with stuff that you can eat, drink, use or exploit. Minimalism is for wimps. Do not knock excess until you have tried it.

When you are consuming heavily and have acquired lots of material things there is a big demand on your leisure time. You need time to enjoy all these things. Nobody would work hard unless they had to. Yet we kid ourselves that workaholics are an honourable crowd. Rubbish. Successful people are **lazy**.

Successful people work the minimum and expend their energies on 'leisure and pleasure' activities. You must be thoroughly and selectively lazy. There are the odd occasions when it is good to work hard, but they are few and far between. If you do have to work hard, do so for the minimum period of time. Work is not good for you. Devote your energies to staying alive, living life to the full and making other people generate your wealth. Apart from that, be as lazy as possible.

I have hinted at a few techniques for being more self centred and explained the rationale. Later we will look at specific techniques and examples for developing world-class skills in self-centredness. Before I do, you need to be aware that looking after number one is great, but there are people out there who want to see you fail. Before we get too self-indulgent we better make sure we minimise their chances of success, especially because their success is likely to be at our expense.

#2 Wield your power

Five ways to be formidable

"Surely the best way to meet the enemy is head on in the field and not to wait until they plunder our very homes?" Oliver Goldsmith

Powerful people use force and in doing so are tough to deal with. Tough people are **demanding, rude, argumentative, critical and aggressive**. By developing these traits you will have five ways to make yourself tougher. Being tough means you can influence others easily and make sure you neutralise opposition before it gathers momentum.

Think of being **demanding** as essential to your success. Be impatient with time-wasting people and expect everything to be done excessively well.

Raise your volume and slow the speed of your speech so that it sounds like every demand you make has a greater importance. People will hang on your every word. People will really listen hard; even if you are talking nonsense it will sound compellingly important. People will feel forced to listen to you.

Ignore all that rubbish about leadership, empowerment and

team working. This has been written either by people who were too vain to admit that they were successful because they were tough bastards, or by people who have interviewed them and been hoodwinked.

Your life is too short to be run by a committee. You decide what needs to happen, tell people and get them to do it. Make deals happen. It is quicker and easier and if people do not like it, they are no use to you anyway. If you have got the time and energy to spend counselling and developing people, coaching them and worrying about sharing responsibilities around, you are not spending enough time enjoying your success. Make decisions quickly and enforce them. Do not waste any time on anything. Be impatient for your success.

I like to follow the example set by the actress and singer Jennifer Lopez. Her demands make most other celebrity's demands look insignificant. J-Lo, as she liked to be called in November 2003, famously upset Hotel staff with her unreasonable demands when she stayed at the Balmoral Hotel in Scotland when attending the MTV Awards that year.

She and her entourage of more than 100 staff occupied the entire top floor of the Balmoral and for the week that she stayed there, this beautiful prima donna ordered Hotel staff not to speak to her or make eye-contact with her, unless she spoke to them first. This is the same woman who reminded us in one of her pop songs that despite her wealth and fame, she was still just "Jenny from the Block."

$ecret Habit$ of $ucce$$ful Ba$tard$

Some people may object to your demanding nature, just as the staff of the Balmoral Hotel did to J-Lo's behaviour. If they do, just be **rude**. Shout at them and if they still do not get the message, make them feel uncomfortable and ostracise them, if necessary. Make it very clear to everyone that you have made your decision and that they had better jump to it.

If you get the right kind of people around you helping you, they will love the unambiguous direction, clarity of decision-making and sense of purpose that you give them. They will do what it takes not to upset you. They will adapt to what you want and the way you want things to happen.

If they do not, then start treating them with contempt. Make sure that you ignore their contribution, even if it is valid, interrupt them and never be polite when you speak to them. Use their full names when addressing them, followed by a sigh, thereby making the message very clear.

If they do not, then get **argumentative**. Be abrasive and confront them - remind them how things are done 'around here.' If they persist, then turn everything they discuss with you into an argument. Soon they will get fed up disagreeing with you and do it your way. Once they realise they have upset you they will be quicker to agree with you the next time.

If they persist, go for their solar plexus and criticise them mercilessly. Having set others the most unreasonable goals possible you should rightly expect them to be met and be very **critical** if things are not as they should be. If you do not question the status quo, you will make no progress.

$ecret Habit$ of $ucce$$ful Ba$tard$

Criticise the smallest failure aggressively. Find the things that are not making the standard and make public examples of them. Demand continuous improvement at all times. Nothing less will do.

The chances are that most people will fail to live up to your expectations, so save yourself the trouble and assume that this will always be the case. Be brutal when assessing people's efforts. If things have failed, it is their fault, not yours. Whatever the excuses, and there will always be many, whatever the factors beyond their control that they claim as mitigating factors, they deserve to be punished for failure.

One failure episode should be enough for you to condemn the person forever. Once you have done this, make sure everyone else knows how poorly they performed, so that they can avoid the possibility that they too fail. Creating a blame culture, driven by fear of retribution, is how many of the most successful people on the planet have operated, so why re-invent the wheel?

Anyone who is still not doing things your way, fast and to the perfect standards you demand needs your full-frontal assault. Go for the jugular and become **aggressive**.

Be very loud and abusive. Be in a bad mood with them whenever possible and make sure they know it. Most successful people have developed the art of abusing people using the strongest language possible. It disturbs people enormously and has a massive impact on them.

People do not expect 'well-heeled' people like you to swear like a trooper. When they do, it is like being physically assaulted. Develop some withering put downs, crammed with expletives. Fire them like guided missiles when you need to firmly make a point.

Abusing people verbally, if done skilfully, weakens most of the people you confront. However, nothing beats delivering it explosively and unexpectedly.

Add some physicality and the impact is incredible. Start with simple things like throwing small objects at transgressors. Paper balls or a pencil eraser if you are in the office; building materials if you are on-site; beer mats or peanuts if you are in a bar. You can of course use cutlery, condiments or bread rolls if you are eating.

If you are able to get away with it, gently cuffing them round the head as you pass and pretending that it was a friendly gesture works wonders.

If you find direct abuse of others challenging, just throw explosive tantrums. Lose your mind in front of people, destroy something, scream and curse. Whilst it is not necessarily directed at anyone, it is the 'carpet bomb' of toughness. It shows people what you are capable of and warns them off early.

Before you relax and enjoy the spoils of your efforts, be on guard. Despite your new self-assured and tough approach to life, there will be people out there trying to knock you down. You must create a reputation for ruthlessness to leave your strongest competitors trailing in your wake.

#3 Never give up

Five ways to be unstoppable

"It matters not whether you win or lose, what matters is whether I win or lose." Darren Weinberg

People who never give up are ruthless. Ruthless people are **fearless, incisive, determined, unforgiving and cruel**. These traits collectively provide an important weapon in the successful bastard's arsenal.

Deep down everybody feels frightened at times. Adrenalin is a gutsy hormone. It makes our bodies react to fearful situations and encourages 'fight or flight' responses in our nervous systems. It is an essential part of our make-up and has helped us to become the dominant animal on the planet. Use it to your advantage.

Fear stems from insecurity. If you are properly self-centred, the confidence and competitiveness that brings, makes you a fighter not a quitter.

If you are tough and are seen as being so by others, you will naturally cultivate a **fearless** approach to life. Use the adrenalin you produce to fight not to simply run away. Same hormone, different uses - it is your choice.

In times of doubt, which everyone has, remember that there are a lot of successful bastards out there that are less self-assured, weaker, more confused and more predictable than you will ever be. If they can make a success of themselves with their limited talents, so can you.

Most people fail in life's game because they were not sure what they wanted out of it in the first place. If you do not know where you are going, any place will do, as they say. The problem with ending up in any place is that the odds are it is not a place you really want to be. Counter the tendency to be vague about your success objectives by being **incisive**.

You want success and you can define what it means to you easily, quickly and definitively. Do so now. Be direct about what you want, be precise about what it is and then stay focussed on getting it from those around you.

Now you know precisely what you want to have to stay the course. You have to be **determined** to succeed at all costs. Hold onto every opportunity and be persistent to the point of madness. Do whatever it takes and never deviate from your objective. This takes a bit of personal discipline for sure, but it will be worth it. Set your targets high and be unrelenting in getting others to support your goals.

In the highly competitive environment that is life, people who want to win will do whatever it takes. Ask any famous Olympic athlete if they have taken a banned performance enhancing substance at any time and they will deny it. They will do so, until they are found out of course – and then they will say it was in an energy drink they bought in a different country or something. It will not be just the Gold medallist either. It will be everybody in the final at the very least and probably every single competitor.

Even Carl Lewis, the vocal anti-doping multiple gold medallist, took performance enhancing drugs. In 2003, Dr. Wade Exum, the United States Olympic Committee's (USOC) director of drug control administration from 1991 to 2000, gave copies of documents to Sports Illustrated which revealed that some 100 American athletes who failed drug tests and should have been prevented from competing in the Olympics were nevertheless cleared to compete. Among those athletes was Carl Lewis.

It was revealed that Lewis tested positive three times before the 1988 Olympics for pseudoephedrine, ephedrine, and phenylpropanolamine, banned stimulants also found in cold medication, and had been banned from the Seoul Olympics and from competition for six months. The USOC accepted his claim of inadvertent use and overturned the decision.

The positive results occurred at the Olympic Trials in July 1988 where athletes were required to declare on the drug-testing forms "over-the-counter medication, prescription drugs and any other substances you have taken by mouth, injection or by suppository."

"Carl did nothing wrong. There was never intent. He was never told, you violated the rules," said Martin D. Singer, Lewis' lawyer, who also said that Lewis had inadvertently taken the banned stimulants in an over-the-counter herbal remedy. "The only thing I can say is I think it's unfortunate what Wade Exum is trying to do," said Lewis. "I don't know what people are trying to make out of nothing because everyone was treated the same, so what are we talking about? I don't get it."

I think it all the more amusing, considering how Lewis spoke out after coming to second to Ben Johnson, in the 100 Metre sprint at the 1988 Olympics in Seoul, Korea. Johnson was subsequently stripped of his World Record and of his gold medal, both of which were handed to Lewis instead, when Johnson tested positive for performance enhancing drugs.

It is common knowledge that the use of drugs in Olympic competition is widespread. Amazingly, in a survey of athletes some years ago, two thirds anonymously confirmed that they would dope themselves up to win a Gold Medal, even if it would cause their death. Now that is what I call being determined.

Having set unreasonably demanding goals for yourself and those around you and got people doing most of the work for you there will still be a few people around who fail to meet your standards or toe-the-line. To these unfortunates you must be **unforgiving**.

Being unforgiving is a powerful personal asset. Never forgive those who cross you. Do not spend valuable time listening to feeble excuses or assessing how this or that person could improve next time and what punishment is appropriate. Simply write them off like you would a car damaged beyond repair.

If a person's transgressions are serious, you can have some fun brutalising them before you dump them. Just be **cruel** to them.

Develop a rich vein of cruelty and hide it behind formal or informal 'team-building' type activities. Be spiteful and pick on the weak or rebellious at every opportunity. If you have a culture of practical jokes or gossip mongering, make these people your target. They will soon get the message and toe the line or leave your inner circle. FIFO as we successful bastards say. Fit in or fuck off. Either will suffice.

I like Philip Green, the Monaco-based billionaire retail entrepreneur. He knows how to be cruel to people. He delights in upsetting journalists and saves his best cruelty for them:

"I took a journalist to France on the plane once. Known her for a long time. Got to Nice airport. Gave her a ticket home and 100 francs for a coffee. 'That's it,' I said, 'End of journey for you.' She thought she was going to Monaco." Ho, ho.

People's past performance is usually an indication of future behaviour, so once the damage is done, close down the matter and move on. Get better people to help you next time round.

So now you are fearless and incisive. Everyone knows you are determined to succeed and that you will stop at nothing to get what you want.

It is now time to exploit your position by undermining your enemies (it is likely you will have a few left from before and one or two that recently appeared) with the forces of unpredictability. If no-one really knows what you are up to, you will soon become a most dominant adversary.

#4 Keep everyone guessing

Five ways to be unpredictable

"I either want less corruption or more chance to participate in it." Ashleigh Brilliant

Staying one step ahead requires judicious use of your cloak and dagger. You need to be a person of mystery and intrigue, difficult for others to judge. You need to keep people guessing what your next move will be. You need to be on the edge, prepared to gamble against the odds and keep everyone guessing what your next move will be. You must be **unpredictable**.

Unpredictable people are **enigmatic, deceptive, unreliable, dishonest and reckless**. Developing these traits will give you that maverick character that will make you difficult to deal with and an impressively mysterious persona that will keep all your enemies panicking about what you are going to do next. Reckless disregard for the laws of the land will allow you to exploit every opportunity for making money and hanging onto it thereafter.

If people know what you are going to do next, that weakens your position. You must be capable of keeping people guessing.

$ecret Habit$ of $ucce$$ful Ba$tard$

Create some mystery in your life and develop an **enigmatic** personality. That is a basic and fundamental requirement of successful people, made into an art form by the successful bastard. If people know you they will better be able to know what you are going to do and they can either copy or potentially worse, sabotage your plans. Keep changing your views and your behaviours, operate with a hint of eccentricity and above all be very secretive, letting no-one know what is really on your mind.

All successful bastards are exceptionally good at getting unfair advantages. To continue to be a winner, you have to be **deceptive**.

You have to deceive people to be successful, you have to take other people's ideas and capitalise on them, even if you are not supposed to, and you have to use whatever they use and more.

You might get lucky, and win once or twice on pure merit, but to keep momentum you have to cheat. Other competitors are cheating, so you must as well to keep pace. Keep yourself utterly, squeaky clean and you will lose. You will usually get away with it and if you are caught out, the penalties will be worth the risks.

Since everyone is at it, who cares. All you are doing is doing what everyone else is doing and where is the harm in that? Why box with one hand tied behind your back? If you are going to box, you need both hands to stand a fair chance. Everyone cheats and successful people cheat everyone.

When you are powerful and in charge, you can forget about all the constraints that normal people assume are essential to success. You can happily be **unreliable** because someone else will always cover for you.

I know how one of the richest men in the world, Larry Ellison, the founder of Oracle Corporation, the software giant, operates first hand. He gets briefings at the very last minute, everyone around him covers up for his lack of interest in things like being on time, or even turning up at all.

I was always told that regardless of the level of importance of a meeting, Larry was not guaranteed to turn up. On a whim, he would decide something else was more important, even if to our team, it was a critical meeting. This 'something else' might have been an attractive air hostess on his flight to London or a new toy like a McLaren F1 motor-car being seen in a showroom on his way from the airport to the office in London.

Nobody was ever upset about Larry's behaviour. After all he was entitled to do what he wanted. Not even very senior customer executives were bothered if he did not turn up to a meeting. In some ways it was better if he did not, because no-one had to worry about incurring his displeasure for something not going well or working perfectly whilst he was in the meeting. He was the boss and everyone knew it. He was, and still is, something to behold.

$ecret Habit$ of $ucce$$ful Ba$tard$

You might think that being a liar, for example, would expose you to all sorts of potential trouble. I used to as well. Until, that is, I joined the ranks of the most incorrigible liars known to man – professional salespeople.

I also know many successful people at every level of social and business life that lie all the time. It is not just salespeople. You will know a few liars yourself for sure. We find out about them when they slip up or when someone else decides it is time to get at them. Bankers, business people, politicians and celebrities are found out all the time. Read the tabloid newspapers on any Sunday.

We all tell white lies. We are late home because of bad traffic, we like the outfit our partner has spent hours getting into, we will get together with someone and we will give them a ring to arrange it, we promise, and so on. We all do it. It is a fact of life.

Lying is utterly pervasive in all professional and political fields and in every home. I have known people who held extremely senior positions that you could tell when they were lying because their lips moved, it really is that prevalent. If you are in any doubt just think, "Bill Clinton" who famously lied under oath by convincing himself that fellatio did not constitute a sexual relationship.

$ecret Habit$ of $ucce$$ful Ba$tard$

I have met Bill Clinton and I can tell you that he is without doubt one of the most charismatic people in the world and for these reasons people forgive him for his inadequacies. People recognise that he is a human being and he needed to lie, just as we all do at times.

If you want to be very successful, get very good at lying. If you do it enough you will soon believe all your own lies and they will become reality. Once they become indistinguishable from reality, you can move onto creating bigger and more complex falsehoods.

Using self-created complex falsehoods and creating the best impression of yourself with others involves believing in yourself so totally that you can convince yourself that things that never happened really did.

The richest people on the planet have mastered lying to the point that it is only when something criminal is detected and doggedly pursued do they get found out. Read any unauthorised biography and you will see what I mean.

Ask any successful person whether they have done anything dishonest to get where they are and they will deny it. You know they have, they know they have, but they will lie until they are blue in the face rather than admit it. They live the lie so well, and so thoroughly, that it becomes indistinguishable from the truth and therefore inconsequential.

$ecret Habit$ of $ucce$$ful Ba$tard$

Which leads me onto the real jewel – being **dishonest** – doing something that most people would perceive as criminally wrong – whether the law would deem it to be or not. As I have said before, if people told the truth, you would know that successful bastards establish criminal activity at the root of their success.

It is a question of degree of course. Some success is based simply on evading and exploiting laws through 'loopholes'. Successful bastards move themselves, their money, businesses, workers and production sites around the world, and use impenetrable labyrinths of off-shore tax havens, holding companies and blind trusts, so that even the best financial sleuth would need a lifetime of investigation to find the truth. 'Blind Trust' is a contradiction in terms as good as 'Military Intelligence' if you ask me.

Overstatement of value of companies is the norm; creation of false revenues and the hiding of costs are the staple diet of all financial controllers. You hear about Enron, Tyco, Adelphia, WorldCom, BCCI, Cendant, HealthSouth, ImClone Systems, Wall Street Banks, Arthur Andersen and so on because they are big and spectacular failures. What you might not know, is that everyone does it. It is normal practice. In a competitive environment, everyone does what is needed to win and companies are just a collection of people and some other assets after all.

$ecret Habit$ of $ucce$$ful Ba$tard$

Unsurprisingly, considering all the challenges of maintaining and enhancing their position, successful bastards live **reckless** lifestyles. They are risk-takers by nature and live life on the edge. They could not survive if they were not. They could not seize opportunities if they did not operate at the boundaries.

The fact that risk is a daily exposure in successful people's live and because they enjoy the excitement of taking risks and winning, their lifestyles orientate towards risky activities. They need the adrenaline rush in every dimension of their lives. Once you get hooked on adrenaline and other powerful neuro-secretions, there is nothing that can match it. Well nothing that exactly matches it.

Most successful bastards abuse themselves; they will push themselves to their limits. To be a paid-up member of this exclusive club you must abuse yourself too, otherwise you will be treated with suspicion.

There are so many opportunities to enhance the life experience and successful bastards want to try them all. It is no wonder that they will consume vast quantities of mind-altering substances, starting with alcohol and tobacco, moving onto harder and more risky recreational pharmaceuticals.

Fast cars, boats and planes will provide extra opportunities for the junkie's fix. No point in having those if do not then drive or pilot them like a lunatic. Danger is joy to the successful person. Dangerous sports attract them like moths to light. Dangerous liaisons are also high on their shopping list.

$ecret Habit$ of $ucce$$ful Ba$tard$

The highly successful are highly sexed. This is because they experience more opportunity with and availability of beautiful people than normal people do, coupled with the hormonal power-station that drives them. Power and money breed sexual opportunity. It is got nothing to with good looks.

Most successful bastards are outrageously behaved when it comes to sex. Being promiscuous is a must for most successful bastards. Maybe there are successful people who have Golden Wedding Anniversaries, but they are few and far between. Most have multiple spouses and multiple sexual partners, the latter simultaneously, the former every few years.

For successful bastards to really get the kicks they need, they need to bring people along with them. They need their support primarily, but their adulation critically boosts their egos to the required level.

Successful bastards fundamentally do not care about other people, so whilst people might feel like they are under their wing, they are not - they are in danger. The successful bastard will take great pleasure transferring their love of risk to those around them and they endanger others in the process. They want others to feel the benefits they do and the rush they do. But as selfish people, they also expect them to take the pain as well. If you are hanging on to some successful bastard's coat-tails, get off and get someone on yours instead.

$ecret Habit$ of $ucce$$ful Ba$tard$

If you doubt me, just remember that King Fahd, the late ruler of Saudi Arabia travelled everywhere with a live human heart donor should he ever need the emergency heart transplant that he feared he would need due to his having been weakened by disease, no doubt brought on by his excessive life-style. He also had a fully staffed operating theatre in every place he went, including in his homes, on his Jumbo jet and on his super-yacht, so he would never have the indignity of an ambulance ride to a nearby hospital.

By now you will be prepared for the work ahead. You know of so many people around you who have used the four habits without you realising it and will see their potential use for your benefit. Now it is your turn. It is time to get into the nitty-gritty of what it really takes to become a successful bastard and see how some of the most well-known people in the world operate.

Look after number one – Being Self-Centred

"Life is either a daring adventure, or nothing." Helen Keller

Be confident	Be sure of yourself	Be clever	Stay cool under pressure	Look smart	Stay aloof
Be competitive	Be ambitious	Seize opportunity	Play to win	Change the rules to suit you	Change the game to suit you
Be selfish	Do what you want	Seek attention for yourself	Take all the credit	Be mean	Never share anything
Be greedy	Get everything you want	Get the best	Get more than you need	Think big	Consume heavily
Be lazy	Only do what you must	Delegate	Avoid hard work	Work part-time	Take lots of holidays

Building Self-Confidence

Techniques to make you more confident

"Confidence is a habit that can be developed by acting as if you already had the confidence you desire to have." Brian Tracy

Be sure of yourself

"The longer I live the more I see that I am never wrong about anything, and that all the pains I have so humbly taken to verify my notions have only wasted my time." George Bernard Shaw

Be sure of yourself. Extend your assertiveness into arrogance. The dividing line is so thin that no-one will notice. Understate it if you like, but do not be afraid to act masterfully as the indispensable genius you so clearly are.

$ecret Habit$ of $ucce$$ful Ba$tard$

Everyone is good at something, known what your something is. Even if you think you are unskilled you are not. Maybe you are good at watching TV. So are TV reviewers. Maybe you are good at drinking. So are Publicans. Maybe you are good at crosswords, good at stacking shelves, good at spotting errors in newspapers, good at making people laugh. Whatever it is, it is a skill and something that you can exploit to your advantage.

How many times have you known you were right to say or do something, but because you lacked confidence you gave in and did not say what you wanted to? You did not trust your expertise. Afterwards, you kicked yourself for not having the courage to speak up and you then spent ages trying to repair the situation to your advantage. In future say what you think and do what you feel.

Use Jose Mourhino, the football club manager, as a role model. Anyone who can nickname himself "The Special One," and subsequently get the traditionally vicious British press to regularly call him that, must be very sure of himself. Being special led to the rather special payoff of £17 million for Jose when he was terminated by Chelsea Football Club when his relationship with owner Roman Abramovich broke down.

Like Jose, you know instinctively when you are right. Develop that gut feel. Remember it is gut feel, not heart feel or head feel. Deep and core beliefs register in the nervous system of the gut, not the heart or the brain. Once your gut is behind you, so to speak, you have no need to doubt any decision you make.

There was a joke circulating in the 1990's around Oracle

Corporation about Larry Ellison, Oracle's founder and CEO that sums up a man being sure of himself most perfectly:

Q: What's the difference between God and Larry Ellison?

A: God doesn't think he's Larry Ellison.

This question amazingly became the title of Larry's *authorised* biography, so there is a clue there somewhere about how far you can take your own self-confidence if you want to be very successful.

For study purposes, watch anyone who has made a ridiculous amount of money in a short space of time or the manager of any top class professional sports team.

Be clever

"The secret of success is to know something that no-one else knows." **Aristotle Onassis**

The difference between being clever and intelligent is that clever people know what to do with what intelligent people know. Surround yourself with intelligent people, not clever people. Then you will stand out. If you are not sure about something ask a clever person. You will get the right answer, unless you are competing, in which case they will lie

Being clever has got nothing to do with IQ. The average IQ is 100. 75% of the population is between 90 and 110. I am 140, by the way, but as my father-in-law reminds me, I am just good at doing IQ tests. I am sure his opinion might have something to do with the fact that he finds them difficult, but I tend to agree with him.

My brother-in-law, Tony Newton, is a greengrocer turned gardener. He does not have a high IQ, and he left school at 14, but he is the cleverest person I know. He knows the value of everything, has a fantastic eye for a deal, is a superb judge of character and he controls and uses his money more wisely than anyone. He has a roguish manner and always has plenty of money. I asked him once if he was printing his own and he pulled out a wad of notes from his pocket, offered them to me and said, "You tell me."

There is no need to be well-educated, just to develop your ability to realise the value of stuff – information, relationships and things.

The list of famous and wealthy people that dropped out of college because they had better things to do is very long. Do not waste time being educated by people who because they cannot do, teach instead. Many of the big-hitters dropped out of college to pursue building their businesses instead, or never even bothered to go in the first place.

You need to know a little of what is worth knowing and

nothing of what is not. You need to be clever. Do not waste time on all the finer detail of knowledge. Find the lowest common denominators and use your intuition.

Being an intellectual snob might well allow you to recognise the William Tell Overture and not shout out "The Lone Ranger" when asked what it is, but it will not be very useful information in the big scheme of things.

Make sure you know the details of important things. The key word is 'know.' Data is the basis of information and when information has a use it becomes knowledge.

You do not need to all the data, just the important information. Get to the hub of any issue that presents itself, find out the data that answers the key questions and use this to improve your position.

Tony Blair, the ex-Prime Minister of Britain stayed in power by surrounding himself with people who were experts in extracting key information from data and then delivering it to him as knowledge. He valued such people very highly. In 2004, he even supported an ex-Cabinet Minister of his called Peter Mandelson, a widely disliked man who had been twice disgraced by scandal, bringing him back from political exile by offering him the job of European Commissioner when it was Britain's year to head the Commission.

Like Mr Blair, always seek the key information that can be used to make an intellectual point or gain a competitive advantage. Use the knowledge gained as a weapon. Once you know what others do not, you are in a position of considerable power and advantage.

$ecret Habit$ of $ucce$$ful Ba$tard$

Ask people questions where you know the answer and you know they do not. That is the pinnacle of cleverness.

I worked as a director for Cisco Systems Inc in the UK and that company is full of very clever managers driving a very clever culture. This giant of the global technology industry has built a fantastic business by creating a numbers focussed culture that is unique in an industry already famed for being obsessed with such things. Senior executives persistently question sub-ordinates about business related numbers, until the respondents are unable to answer accurately and they suffer significant embarrassment as a result.

This simple 'trick' creates an environment where everyone feels compelled to know everything about their area of the business, not only the data, but the deeper meaning of it as well, or risk facing public humiliation if they do not. This behaviour ripples down through the company to all levels of employee and makes everyone pay great attention to the detailed numbers relating to their piece of the business. Coupled with a thrice weekly sales forecasting and commitment process, and a painful haranguing for anyone who misses any such commitment, it drives the most incredible work-rate amongst the entire workforce.

Having been on the inside at Cisco Systems, it is no surprise to me why in the boom of the 1990's they were the largest company in the world by market capitalisation or why they continue to be one of the most successful companies ever. It is a good chance that Cisco will be the greatest and biggest technology company in the world one day soon, thanks to the clever people that run it.

110

Stay cool under pressure

Do NOT get stressed-out about anything. Do not worry or get depressed. Look relaxed and comfortable at all times. It helps if you do not think too hard about what is happening around you if you want to stay cool. Imagine you are non-stick, Teflon-coated and impervious to injury.

Most people get stressed because they make themselves too busy; they take on too much in too little time. Play things by ear, see how the cookie crumbles, see how the wind blows, 'shoot the breeze' a little.

I love the story Donald Trump recalls in one of his many books. He was walking in New York City in the early 1990's when he had accumulated insurmountable debt and was facing potential bankruptcy at the hands of his creditors. He passed a vagrant on the sidewalk and Trump recalls thinking, "He was worth $9.2 billion more than I was." 'The Donald' as he is known survived the spectre of bankruptcy, restructured his financial affairs and moved on.

In 2006, his finance people estimated his net worth to be $4.2 billion. Today, he is now more famous, wealthy and popular than ever, thanks in part to his TV show, "The Apprentice" which earns him reportedly $3M per episode, which is a nice bit of pocket money for what he describes as his 'hobby.'

So if you think your overdraft is a bit high, stay cool and deal with it. Most really wealthy people owe more than you will earn in your lifetime. They use other people's money to make more for themselves.

For study purposes watch any Poker professional that has won a World Title or any billionaire, anytime.

Look smart

If you want to be successful, you must first look successful. Buy fewer, but more expensive clothes and look after them. If you are going to wear jewellery, wear one or two pieces and make them the best you can afford. Start with a watch; add a ring and that is usually enough. Too much jewellery will make you look ridiculous, a target for muggers and will distract people you are trying to influence, so do not fall into that trap.

$ecret Habit$ of $ucce$$ful Ba$tard$

Be well-groomed and develop the skill of looking smart in casual wear. Most people look like paupers when they dress down. This will do you no good. Keep some very special items for those casual days.

Be like Sven Goran Eriksson, the legendary multi-millionaire football manager and the only man to have won the league-and-cup double in three different countries (Sweden, Portugal and Italy)

He reportedly has around 150 hand-tailored suits in his wardrobe. "Sven takes pride in his appearance and has a collection of very expensive bespoke suits that he has built up over the years," a club source told one tabloid.

A rumour in the game that he buys one every time he beds a new girlfriend is apparently unfounded.

For study purposes look any of the many lists of best dressed people that are published in glossy magazines, anyone who is going for an important job interview that has a chance of getting it, or watch any TV or Film awards ceremony. You could also watch any billionaire, any time, unless he is Warren Buffet.

Stay aloof

"Nothing affects me. And nothing affects the way I think of myself." Donald Trump

When you are a successful bastard, you look down on the masses of people yet to discover how to become one. You also look down on people who will criticise, complain and try to compete with you.

Look down your nose at people. If you find this difficult, get yourself a pair of designer glasses with small lenses and just perch them on the end of your nose. If you are over fifty years old, get a pair with half-lenses. They will remind you what to do more easily.

Another good, but slightly more expensive, way to remind yourself how aloof you are is to get a luxurious penthouse at the top of a landmark building in a big city.

I hope one day to have something like "The Donald" has. His home occupies the top three floors of Trump Tower on 5th Avenue in New York City.

It helps you to believe in yourself when you have a $50M apartment, on the top three floors of a tower named after you, bedecked in gold, bronze and marble, offering 30,000 square feet (3,000 m²) to bounce around and count your money in.

$ecret Habit$ of $ucce$$ful Ba$tard$

One of the most successful bastards of all time that stayed aloof throughout his whole life was Myer Lansky, the shadowy founding Godfather of the American Mafia. Myer was the brains and the financier and someone every Mafioso listened to. His partner in crime, 'Lucky' Luciano, once said of Lansky, that "the barrel of his gun was curved," in reference to the fact that he was always outside the line of fire.

Throughout Lansky's 50 year reign he was never convicted, in fact he has a cleaner record than the President of the USA, George Bush Jnr. Lansky did not spend one day in prison despite being doggedly pursued by law enforcement agencies for five decades. He died peacefully at his Miami home in 1983, reportedly leaving an estate of more than $400M, not one dollar of which has ever been located.

For study purposes watch any small town Magistrate, anyone who is senior Mason or anyone who is making enormous sums from corrupt business activity. It may save you time if this is all one and the same person.

Before you move onto building your competitive skills, get firmly grounded and really believe in yourself. You are special, you must not get weighed down with complex detail when some key facts are best, act relaxed at all times and dress smartly whilst you rise far above everyone around you.

Becoming a key player

Techniques to make you more competitive

"I play to win, whether during practice or a real game. And I will not let anything get in the way of me and my competitive enthusiasm to win." Michael Jordan

Be ambitious

"Do not stay in bed, unless you can make money in bed."
George Burns

Someone who is ambitious has a strong desire for success and for most people this means getting lots of power and wealth. You would not be reading this book if you did not have at least some desire to be more successful, indeed you are probably very ambitious.

Some people, usually the failures, dislike ambition and see it is a negative characteristic of people. That is, of course, bullshit

$ecret Habit$ of $ucce$$ful Ba$tard$

spread by successful bastards themselves. They keep the masses under control by stifling individual ambition.

Ambition is what makes dreams reality. Ambition is the driving force that enables people reach their goals. Ambition is based not on a vague wish, it is a decision.

If you do not know where you are going, any road will do, as they say. Know what you want and it will make life much easier. If you know what you want and where you want to be, ambition gets you there.

Set clear goals for yourself, make them public and go for it. Your goals must be tangible and time-bound, and above all simple. They should be something like:

- Big house by 25

- New Ferrari by 30

- Two kid family by 35

- Retirement by 40.

Make the ambitions real commitments, not a wish list. If they are real, you will be forced to do some things seriously to make them happen. Make them real and some good things will follow:

(1) People will ask you how you are going to achieve them

(2) You will be forced to figure out how

(3) You will have to make big efforts achieve them.

Do not worry about being overly ambitious. If you are, you will get farther than by being moderately ambitious. Tell your boss that you want his/her job and ask them when you can have it. If they do not tell you, ask your boss's boss.

Better still, resign, take what you know with you and create your own business doing the same thing, but better. It is the only way to make real money.

For study purposes watch the eldest child of any successful entrepreneur after they are appointed CEO of the family corporation whilst still in their early twenties.

Seize opportunity

"Carpe diem." Horace

Look at everything in terms of the opportunity presented to you. Get your opportunity radar switched onto the 'sensitive' setting.

$ecret Habit$ of $ucce$$ful Ba$tard$

Opportunities will be can be classified into three types. Every opportunity will relate to one or more of the following, and ideally all three:

- Money

- Exposure

- Enjoyment.

Assess every situation in terms of these and quickly assess the return you will get for the effort you put in. If it does not feel worthwhile instantly, do not pursue it.

One of our best loved entrepreneurs and businessmen is Sir Richard Branson. Sir Richard seizes opportunity, especially if it includes some gratuitous self-promotion, like no-one else.

When British Airways decided to discontinue flying Concorde, Branson was immediately on the Government's case, offering to pay £1 each for the supersonic birds that remained in service, highlighting that this was what British Airways had effectively paid the UK Government when the company was privatised. He even had Concorde models constructed with the Virgin Atlantic logo positioned prominently on them on display on his desk when interviewed at the time for television news.

Whether Branson truly intended to take on the loss-making and hugely expensive fleet of ageing aircraft is not known, but he did not miss the opportunity to get one over on his major competitor at that time by saying that he did. You too should seize every opportunity, even if you do not really want it – you never know where it might lead.

Play to win

Show me a good loser and I will show you someone who does not win very often. The joy in winning is something that winners know well and losers have no clue about. Until you win, you think that it is ok just to have played and you cannot see what all the fuss is about. Once you start winning you will get a life-long taste for it, I promise you. Start today.

The greatest golfer in the world, Tiger Woods, is arguably the most competitive man alive. His mastery of one of the most difficult sports known to man, means he personifies competitiveness perfectly:

"I don't look at what the purse is or the prize money. You play. And when you play, you play to win, period. That's how my dad raised me; you go out there and win. If you win, everything will take care of itself. You take great pride in what you do on the golf course, and when you're able to win events, that's when you can go home and be very proud of what you've done." Tiger Woods

Be like Tiger, be committed to winning. Be committed to beating others. Otherwise, what is the point in competing in the first place?

$ecret Habit$ of $ucce$$ful Ba$tard$

Stop being embarrassed if you continuously beat someone. Simply find a stronger opponent. Look at being competitive as a healthy and character-building pastime.

Everything you do is a competition of one sort or another. Your position in life itself is as a competitor in a giant game. Millions of people are playing against you, competing for what you deserve, so you should hone your competitive skills if you want to win.

In every activity, look for opponents. If you cannot spot any easily, compete with yourself. Push yourself above the norm and excel in everything you do.

I used to work with currency traders in the City of London and these people are the masters of competition. They would wager bets on everything imaginable to promote the competitive environment. They would even bet on which raindrop would hit the bottom of the window first as they ran down the office window pane. Follow their examples and use wagers to increase the intensity of competition.

Be the highest paid, the fastest promoted, the person with most knowledge and authority, the driver of the best car, the owner of the best house. Above all, compete and be the best.

Do not bother with autopsies should you lose. You will just upset yourself. Pretend it did not happen. Better still, avoid losing altogether by making and changing the rules to suit you.

For study purposes, watch bookmakers at the race-track, anyone who trades high volumes of anything.

Change the rules to suit you

A good friend of mine, Andy Baulch, a licensed London Taxi driver and my personal chauffeur, is the most naturally competitive individual I know. Andy is a joy to behold in competition. He thrives on it. He wins so often at everything he attempts, particularly at sports, that he can rightfully claim in my circle to be the master of competition.

Andy has developed a sixth sense for extending competitions and changing the rules when he realises that things might not go his way. From the simple "best of three" darts match that somehow becomes the "best of 21" as his opponent outplays him early on, through to the creation of competitions within the competition to make sure he can win.

If Andy is betting on the outcome of a round of golf, for example, he will add new sub-wagers on the outcome of specific shots and holes as soon as he sees the chances of winning the whole match fade. Whatever happens, he finishes victorious somehow.

For study purposes, watch licensed London Taxi Drivers on the golf course.

Change the game to suit you

If you really want to be mega-successful, change the game itself. Swap to another way of money-making, introduce major changes to the current one, or invent a new one altogether.

Most of my experience in business has been in the field of technology and that industry is a game changer extraordinaire. Who would have thought that any company could put a camera in a phone and everyone who has one to take videos and load them onto their own website ten years ago? Now this is one of the most profitable and fastest growing business areas in the world.

You can change the game, even if at a smaller level, it will have great impact. You know you have some really special skills. There are some things you really excel at, and you do so effortlessly and naturally. You will find that the things you excel at doing are also the things you most enjoy doing. That is because you are good at them and you therefore perform well, which makes you feel good about yourself.

What are the three things that you are the best at doing? Numbers, public speaking, telling jokes, reading fast, acting the fool, listening, saving money, dealing with people..... They could be anything, but think hard to come up with those that are the undisputed top three.

Now, armed with this insight about yourself, think how you can use these skills more in your day-to-day money-making efforts. Get more involved in those parts of your life where your skills have the most positive impact on you. Change your job role to be more suited to your skills, change your professions if necessary.

The people who make fortunes change the way something is made or experienced. They change the game in their favour and as prime movers in the new environment they have an opportunity to flourish before potential competitors can prepare themselves.

For study purposes, watch anyone who works at a senior level with really advanced technology and gets away with looking like someone living on welfare handouts.

Getting what you want

Techniques to make you more selfish

"Selfishness is not living as one wishes to live; it is asking others to live as one wishes to live." Oscar Wilde

Do what you want

"Begin doing what you want to do now. We are not living in eternity. We have only this moment, sparkling like a star in our hand-and melting like a snowflake..." Francis Bacon Sr

Instead of saying "I have to" do something, say "I choose to" do something. If it feels wrong, you should not be doing it. If it feels right, then carry on.

Most people actually do what they want, most of the time, but convince themselves that others are making them do it. How much of what you did today felt like free choice.

The "I choose to" technique will help you spot the things that others are making you do and you can eliminate them from your

schedule. Try saying, "No," to people more often. It works
wonders.

Seek attention

*"The nice thing about egotists is that they do not talk about
other people." Lucille S Harper*

Be an attention seeker. Get people focused on you and what
you say about yourself. The easiest way to do this is to talk
about yourself all the time.

Make sure that as much of every conversation is about you.
Regardless of the subject, relate it directly to your experience
alone and hold the conversation entirely around your amazing
exploits in life.

Save your best efforts for when someone is talking about
what they have done and people seem interested. Without
hesitation state they you have done the same thing but more of
it, better, more often, more recently and more successfully.

The key words to remember are "I," "me" and "my." Use
them gratuitously. Make these words longer by stretching them
out whilst talking, and over emphasise them heavily. If possible
use them all in a single sentence as often as possible. It is not
easy, but with practice it will come.

$ecret Habit$ of $ucce$$ful Ba$tard$

If you are ever stuck, simply start a sentence with one of the three key words and the rest will follow. If you have to pause while you think about the rest of the sentence, simply elongate the first word until you are ready.

Try some phrases like, "I think my qualifications alone tell you enough about me," when you are faced with that probing question in a job interview.

Maybe even a little self-deprecation can be slipped in, after one of your jokes falls flat or you make a clumsy mistake - "I do make me laugh, even if I say so myself"

Accomplished "I, me, my" people will also develop the ability to use the words "you," "they," "them," "him" and "her" in sentences inaudibly, by shortening them so severely that all one hears is a muffled grunt where the word should be. This allows even more emphasis on the "I, me, my" words, which is all that is important anyway.

If you happen to be Royal, simply swap "One" for both "I" and "Me" and "One's" for "My."

For study purposes, watch anyone who seeks out unreasonable self-publicity or someone who has never experienced business failure or personal hardship since making their first million at the age of 19.

Take all the credit

*"It is always been and always will be the same in the world:
The horse does the work and the coachman is tipped."* **Anon**

Taking all the credit involves doing two things well. Both depend on you knowing what is going well and what is going badly.

Use a phrase like, "I have never been associated with failure," when briefing workers, partners or senior management and they will get the message that you will never admit you are wrong and you will blame everyone but yourself if things fail.

I remember when the Accident Group (TAG) personal claims company collapsed in the UK in 2003. Mark Langford the multi-millionaire founder of the 'ambulance chasing' company left it to the administrators to sack his 2,500 staff by SMS text message.

The first message to staff to, "check your e-mail for salary news," was followed swiftly by, "Unfortunately salaries not paid – please do not contact the office – full details to follow later."

Langford, who enjoyed the trappings of success with a fortune of over £40M and a Cheshire mansion set in a 25-acre estate with a lake and indoor pool, plus a villa in Spain and a fleet of luxury cars, claimed his hands were tied saying, "If I could have sorted everything out I would have. I care passionately about my people." When workers demanded that he pay them out of his accumulated wealth, he claimed it had all gone in the crash. When reporters tried to contact him at his Spanish villa, a maid told them he was not there, giving us another great example of a rich and successful bastard not prepared to shoulder the blame, but happy to take all the 'credit.'

Associate yourself with lots of projects and distance yourself from anything that fails. If something fails, it is not your fault and you cannot be held accountable. When things succeed, make sure you write the press release or internal report. Exaggerate your involvement in the successes and remove any evidence of being involved in failures.

For study purposes, watch any male American executive that has his initials on his shirt and tassels on his shoes, any female American executive that wears red suits or any entrepreneur that made their money 'managing' risks.

Be mean

"There are plenty of ways to get ahead. The first is so basic I'm almost embarrassed to say it: spend less than you earn."
Paul Clitheroe

Always say you give donations to charity anonymously,

$ecret Habit$ of $ucce$$ful Ba$tard$

because you say, you do not want the publicity. That way, no one will know that you have not given anything. When you have made and established your fortune and there is no way you can spend it all, then you can become a philanthropist, but in the meantime:

Do not carry large amounts of money with you

Do not make large cash withdrawals

Avoid credit cards that do not insist you pay them back each month. Paying interest should be a crime.

Shop around for everything

Haggle over the price of everything

Studiously avoid buying drinks and meals for anyone but yourself.

There are of course exceptions, but these are only reserved for when you are trying to impress others. Lavish parties and expensive entertainment are all very much allowed, but only when the guest list includes people who will subsequently be of use to you.

$ecret Habit$ of $ucce$$ful Ba$tard$

When Sir Philip Green, the billionaire retail entrepreneur, spends tens of millions on his son's Bar Mitzvah, or his own 50th birthday party, this is only because when you look at the guest list, it includes some of the most famous and influential people in his sphere of business. His generosity has a purpose. He does not invite the people that make him all those millions, working in his shops on the near minimum wage or sweating in Third world countries to produce the garments he sells.

The most legendary miser yet greatest philanthropist in later life has to be Warren Buffett, the billionaire US investor and head of Berkshire Hathaway, worth an estimated US$52 billion in 2007, is reported to have lent his daughter Susie $20 to get her car out of the airport garage, but made her write him a cheque there and then to pay him back.

For study purposes, watch anyone who successfully supports a large family and pays a mortgage on their own home, whilst earning close to the national minimum wage, or any billionaire.

Never share anything

"He, who shareth honey with the bear, hath the least part of it." Proverb

Ownership is everything. With ownership comes the authority to make important decisions, craft things your way and above all to get the benefits derived by whatever it is you own.

If the object is a money-making venture you want to realise the profits from your endeavours, not line someone else's pockets.

Never ever share your business with anyone. Most partnerships collapse when people eventually fall out with one another, so do it alone.

For study purposes, watch anyone who has been involved in a failed business partnership or bankrupt family business, or currently owns a business that operates only in a far-off country than the one they reside in.

Getting more of what is good for you

Techniques to make you greedier

"Greed is all right; by the way I think greed is healthy. You can be greedy and still feel good about yourself." Ivan F. Boesky

Get everything you want

"Becoming wealthy is like playing Monopoly... the person who can accumulate the most assets wins the game." Noel Whittaker

I am amazed at how so many people feel guilty about satisfying their desire for material things. There is no point in having wealth if you do not spoil yourself with it. If you want something, get it. Get everything you want.

My friends often comment on my shoe collection, watches and

hand-made suits, my collections of art, my cars and my houses. They always do this in a positive, albeit slightly amazed, kind of way. They never think I am being stupid or wasting my money. They know it is mine and I do with it what I want. They just find it amazing that I can have so much beautiful stuff.

One of the best exponents at having everything he wants is Elton John, the fabulously successful musical entertainer. He has apartments, mansions and villas around the world and they are decorated in the most beautiful and expensive way imaginable.

On one occasion when he was in court litigating against his accountants for not keeping track of his wealth to his satisfaction, it came to light that he had spent £293,000 on cut flowers in an 20 month period from January 1996. The opposing barrister, in an attempt to show Elton as a man of ridiculous excess, asked him how he could justify spending this fantastic amount. Elton replied simply, "I like flowers."

If you like flowers, or hats, or cars, or racehorses or powerboats or whatever, just get them. Get everything you want, you deserve it.

Get the best

Surround yourself with the best and most amazing things. Be a fully committed materialist. It is your wealth, for you to enjoy.

Only buy the best things. They look better and last longer and have a lower lifetime cost. There is one wonderful aspect of being able to buy nice things. You can enjoy them AND make more money in the process. It is just one superb fringe benefit of a being successful bastard.

If you have lots of money, buying really expensive things can become a real money-spinner, and even a business in its own right. Art, antiques, property and classic motor-cars are just some of the extravagances that will appreciate in value as they get older. Add to that the fact that you are a famous person who once owned them and they will sell at a premium at auction because of it. Ask Elton John.

When Elton sobered up and sold much his collection of art, clothes, furniture and cars after realising that much of it was not to his taste, having been purchased during a lengthy drug and booze fuelled stupor, he managed in most cases to sell the things for more than he had paid for them. How great is that?

When you have beautiful material things, secure them well. Over-insure them, keep the receipts and keep them safely stored. I recommend you keep a detailed asset register so that you can easily prove what you own. Mark the goods in some way so that you can physically prove they are your items should they go astray.

Having your asset register in the form of an annotated electronic photograph album is a great way to store it. This will enable you to show other people what you have without having to go to the trouble of showing them in the flesh. You can show or send the photographs to whoever you want easily and use them to remind yourself of how lucky you are. I like to regularly update my 'screen saver' on my PC to show the best of what I have.

I picked up this technique from a remarkable man called Graham Harrison, a self-made millionaire I had the pleasure of working with who enjoys nothing more than flaunting his possessions. He carries photographs with him of his cars and blueprints and photographs of his houses in his briefcase and would proudly talk you through them at any opportunity. To make sure such opportunity arose, he would leave the pictures scattered on a table in his office, where even the most guarded visitor amongst us felt compelled to make an opening comment about them and unwittingly give him his licence to thrill. My screen-saver is just a more modern version of his desktop.

Graham was strangely even proud of his own hair. He sported a smartly styled full head of hair that was impressive for a man in his mid-fifties. He announced to me one day as he swept out of the office earlier than usual that he was going to have, "the most beautiful and gorgeous haircut in the world."

I wonder to this day whether he kept the hair that was cut off in a little box somewhere or perhaps a few selected photographs of the same somewhere in his briefcase.

For study purposes, just watch any wealthy entertainer or self-made businessman with a really nice hairdo.

Get more than you need

As an ambitious person, you will naturally develop a healthy dissatisfaction with what you have. You will always want more; always want to go one better.

If you cannot afford more, get someone to lend you the money until you have accumulated your own. Robert Earl, the Hard Rock Café founder, was once asked how it felt to be a multi-millionaire after he sold his restaurant chain to Rank Leisure. His response was, "I have always lived like a millionaire - the difference now is that I have the money."

Be like Prince Jefri Bolkei, the brother of the Sultan of Brunei, whose excesses are without doubt the most profligate of anyone in modern history. It is reported that the Prince, prior to being reined in by his brother in the late 1990's, spent more prolifically than any individual, ever. He is reported to have spent up to £8 billion in a mad 10-year spending spree. Much of this huge sum was spent on things that he had no need for and could never use fully and he is alleged to have embezzled all this cash from Brunei state coffers whilst managing the states wealth on behalf of his brother.

$ecret Habit$ of $ucce$$ful Ba$tard$

The Prince was reported to have a multi-million pound town house in Park Lane, next to the Dorchester (which his brother owned) in which he kept a stable of 20 high-class prostitutes, twenty four hours a day, every day, to cater for his every need when he visited the UK just a few times a year. He liked to buy everything in bulk.

Having been brought to heel by his brother, in an out-of-court settlement, Jefri agreed to hand over assets worth £3 billion to the state, including hotels, aircraft and his infamous 180 foot yacht, Tits, along with the yacht's two tenders (no pun intended) Nipple I and Nipple II.

The Sultan also instructed the Prince to sell most of the things that he had bought during his spending spree to try and recoup some of the money he had splashed about.

The resulting auction catalogue covered 21 warehouses full, according to a local businessman, of "very, very super-luxurious" items, including 16,000 tons of Italian marble, tracts of sandalwood and teak, as well as two Mercedes fire trucks, gold bathroom utensils and toilet brushes, crystal chandeliers, a flight simulator for a jumbo jet and ninety UK telephone boxes!

Prince Jefri also liked cars and reportedly he bought more than 2,000 of them over the years. According to one estimate, at his peak, the Prince spent £50m every year on top-of-the-range cars.

When his spending spree was finally curtailed in 1998 and he was sacked as head of his brother's Brunei based investment company, he allegedly owed Rolls-Royce £18m, Mercedes £15m for dozens of customised 600 SL models, £4m to Aston Martin, plus unknown amounts to Porsche, Ferrari and

$ecret Habit$ of $ucce$$ful Ba$tard$

McLaren.

The auditors, Arthur Andersen were sent in search of the cars
he had bought, including six McLaren F1 cars, costing £650,000
each. Many of the hundreds of cars could not be found,
apparently having been given away, broken up and sold by
thieving aids, or simply misplaced. He had simply forgotten
where he had parked them.

You may wonder why he needed six McLaren F1's, but that
was because he was often in the habit of buying several of the
same cars, identical in all but colour, so that he had a different
coloured one to match his mood on any particular day.

Never mind the cars, Jefri also to top it all, in 1996 the Prince
commissioned the largest and most luxurious private yacht ever
to be built. The 160m long vessel, estimated to have cost in
excess of £300M although it was never delivered. The shell was
bought by the ruling family of Dubai and this yacht, now known
as The Dubai, is due to be completed soon having been fitted
out for the last ten years.

So if you think it extravagant to have lots of shoes, watches,
suits, cars or whatever, think again. Think like Prince Jefri.

After being reined in, his generous brother gave him an
allowance of $500K per month, which to you and me would be
a survivable allowance, but the Prince did have 35 children and
three wives, so he obviously found it a tad challenging to live on
such a measly sum. Despite losing his assets and constrained by
his monthly allowance, Jefri has somehow still managed to live
a life of considerable opulence to the present day.

$ecret Habit$ of $ucce$$ful Ba$tard$

His brother the Sultan, understandably pissed off with Jefri, pursued him in the High Court in 2006 demanding he reveal the source of his income or risk facing a prison sentence. Lord Justice Waller agreed that Jefri's lifestyle following the 2001 auction ruled out the possibility that he was simply gaining additional support from wealthy friends and relatives unless, "the prince had won the lottery or had had some good evenings in the casino".

At first, Jefri and his lawyers tried to halt the action, saying any such investigation represented a violation of his human rights under the European Convention. The court were not taken in and Jefri looked like he was heading for the clink until his brother decided that after five years, enough was enough and stopped the court action

For study purposes, watch Royalty or anyone of Middle-Eastern appearance that has five names, including two that are hyphenated or anyone with an Al in their name that is not a shortening of Alan, Albert, Alexander or Alistair.

Think BIG

"You have 50,000 thoughts each day. You might as well make them big ones." Donald Trump

Why waste something as precious as a conscious thought on insignificant things? Think big.

Consume heavily

With all you have you need to experience the joy of abundance fully. You do not see all that many wealthy people looking slim and fit. Their size reflects their status.

Open up the world of gastronomic extravagance. Fine food and fine drink are joyful. Abundance is overwhelming. You will soon build a tolerance for banquets and indulgent mega-parties. As your consumption grows, people will further respect you. You are enjoying what you deserve.

For study purposes, watch any head chef, anyone big in the Corporate Hospitality sector, internationally known Opera singers or anyone who knows a lot about antique pottery.

Making better use of your time

Techniques to make you lazier

"One day recently a man called out to me from the other side of the street asking for the price of a drink. I beckoned him to come over for it and he waved me away. This has to be the Everest of laziness." Jeffrey Bernard

Only do what you must

"I do not want to achieve immortality through my work….. I want to achieve it through not dying." Woody Allen

Try something for me. Write down the three things you MUST do yourself as part of your money making effort.

Be very hard on yourself. They must be things that only YOU can do. Then re-organise your life around these.

I am a writer, so you might think I must need to type well. I do not. Two fingers works just fine. You might think I would have to be brilliant at grammar and punctuation. I am not.

$ecret Habit$ of $ucce$$ful Ba$tard$

Microsoft does the main bit and then I just get my Dad to review the copy and he corrects everything. Many famous authors write terrible prose and it then gets corrected by proof readers and editors.

The one problem with using agents and publishers is that, like venture capitalists, they expect a high return for using their skills and connections. They are also notoriously careful what they invest in.

It is of course okay for J.K. Rowling to demand a large slice of profits because her Harry Potter books, films and merchandise are guaranteed to make money, but most authors get very little for their books when publishing their first work. Even the great Ms Rowling's work was rejected by eight publishers before Bloomsbury made their best decision ever and signed her up.

Sometimes it is better to do the work yourself and keep a bigger slice of the profits. This book for instance, being self-published puts ten times as much in my pocket for every copy sold. Sometimes, it is worth doing it yourself.

For study purposes, watch anyone who has been married more than twice, or has had a life threatening experience more than once. They may of course be one and the same person.

Delegate

"The world is full of willing people, some willing to work, the rest willing to let them."   **Robert Frost**

If you do not have to do it, but it needs to be done, delegate it. Delegation makes a lot of sense. If you do not delegate then it is only your effort that can generate wealth and that limits your potential. Why keep a dog and bark yourself, as they say.

You cannot do everything yourself, so do not try. Successful bastards only do what is necessary themselves, they get others to do the rest.

There are a few choices you can make when presented with something that needs to be done:

You can DO it, DELAY it, DELEGATE it or DUMP it. Never delay it, it will not happen. If you cannot do it because it is not one of your short listed tasks, either dump it or delegate it. I recommend doing both in equal measure.

Develop the ability to present other people's ideas and to do so at short notice after quick briefings.

Some people like to be in the detail because they feel they have to be. David Lloyd, who founded and subsequently sold his eponymous chain of leisure clubs, used to check every set of accounts from every club by hand, and long hand at that. Spreadsheets were not for him. He claims it allowed him to be in complete control of the business. In other words, he could find out if people were fiddling him more easily.

I would prefer to have an accountant or trusted underling doing that for me. However, make sure you carry out some simple checks to make sure they are not stealing from you if you do get someone else to do something for you. If you cannot afford to pay someone trustworthy to do the job for you then do it yourself.

Avoid hard work

"When a man tells you that he got rich through hard work, ask him: 'Whose?'." Don Marquis (1878-1937)

Hard work is bad for you. Work smart not hard. Most of what you do now is probably pointless, so do not stay buried in the overwork trap. If something is too tough, you should not be doing it yourself anyway.

Develop the ability to present other people's ideas as your own by getting someone to brief you on important things just before you need to talk about them. That way you will not waste time learning stuff you will never use again.

For the sake of your sanity, do not become a workaholic. It is pointless. If you can tell me anyone who has said on their deathbed, "I wish I had spent more time at work," I will be willing to rethink this one. Otherwise avoid everything that looks like hard work.

For study purposes, spend some time with someone who is a sleeping partner in a booming business, has invented a game show or who deals in massive quantities of illegal substances.

"I shall do less whenever I shall believe what I am doing hurts the cause and I shall do more whenever I shall believe doing more will help the cause." Abraham Lincoln

Work part-time

At one all-day business meeting I attended a guy arrived at 12-00 after a very heavy session in the hotel bar the night before. Instead of an apology he announced to the team, "Oh, you were obviously not told that I do not do mornings," in response to what he saw of our surprise at his relaxed demeanour. Brilliant.

He totally deflected any criticism and his lateness was ignored by everyone. This is a marvellous technique for allowing you to get away with doing half-days. Just make sure that people know you will not be there and it will be tolerated.

$ecret Habit$ of $ucce$$ful Ba$tard$

If you are not up all night, get in early, before anyone else does. This gives you a chance to get ahead of the game and allows you to quite reasonably take the afternoon off after a long lunch. No-one will know what time you really got in, apart from security, and they can be bribed easily, so everyone will forgive you assuming that you have just decided to work your version of flexible hours. If you are cunning, you can have a leisurely breakfast and a read of the paper as well.

Once you are a really successful bastard, your name and your gems of knowledge and voluminous contact list will be enough to get you a few one-day a month non-executive appointments. These are the cream. You do next to fuck-all, take no responsibility and only have to turn up for a good lunch and a chat a few times a year. You will get paid twice the national average wage for just turning up occasionally, so if you get a few of these they can provide a very nice incremental income for little effort on your part.

Develop some work related activity that allows you to play golf, go to fine restaurants, go to glorious country houses for seminars and generally to places where no-one will know how many hours you work whilst there. Ideally work and play should become indistinguishable.

For study purposes watch anyone who plays a sport professionally.

Take lots of holidays

Everybody loves a holiday. Most people only get one holiday per year, or two if they are lucky. Successful bastards seem to always be going on holiday. They have an all the year round suntan, which clearly has not been the result of a few sessions on a cheap sun-bed.

You are the boss, you do not need to ask for permission or fill in an administrative holiday card to take a break from work. Take holidays frequently. They are good for you.

Successful bastards have holiday homes in places that are sunny all year around. They make a point of letting you know this and of making sure that they get to visit their villa in Portugal, or wherever, at least once a month. They are the sort of people that when you phone them on a Thursday, they answer their mobile with a jaunty and exaggerated, hello, and then proceed to tell you that they are by the beach having a spot of lunch and therefore could they call you back later on.

Even if you are constrained by having only four or five weeks holiday as part of your job, you can easily extend this to 10 weeks or more by taking regular long weekends and claiming the days a time off in lieu of some fictitious over-time that you claim you have worked.

If you are self-employed, independently wealthy or the boss of your own business then the term 'holiday' should have little relevance to you. Every day should be a holiday, with work being a minor distraction.

If you cannot afford lots of holidays, pay the few pounds at your local health club to get on a rapid, high quality sun-bed, and pretend that you have them.

For study purposes, watch anyone who works as a porter in a large flower or fruit and vegetable market or someone who has taken early retirement from the Police Force, ideally through supposed ill-health.

Wield your power – Being Tough

"Lord grant me the serenity to accept the things I cannot change, the courage to change the things I can and the wisdom to hide the bodies of those I had to kill because they pissed me off." **Anon**

Be demanding	Be impatient	Expect the unachievable	Be unreasonable	Be bossy	Be inflexible
Be rude	Be abrupt	Be ignorant	Be patronising	Put people down	Never be polite
Be argumentative	Be abrasive	Be confrontational	Turn every discussion into an argument	Make mountains out of molehills	Win every argument
Be critical	Be pedantic	Criticise immediatley	Focus on the negative	Ignore input	Make your criticism personal
Be aggressive	Be loud	Be abusive	Be bad-tempered	Be physical	Be explosive

Achieving the impossible

Techniques to make you more demanding

"Perfection is our goal, excellence will be tolerated." **Anon**

Be impatient

You are not here for long and time is precious. Your impatience reflects your desire to get things done your way, fast, so be as impatient as you like, as often as you like.

Time wasting is a crime and if it is your time being wasted you must deal with the culprit swiftly and brutally. Demand things are done quickly. Forget about perfection, just get the job done and finished as best as possible in the shortest time.

When dealing with a time waster, imagine that you are going through customs, late for a flight and whoever is talking to you is one of those pesky Customs officials searching for that miniscule nail file inadvertently left in your wash bag that showed up as a tiny blur on their X-ray machine.

Get people's disagreements out early so that you can snuff them out before they gather steam.

Expect the unachievable

Teamwork is when a lot of people do what you say.

Make your orders clear and unambiguous – what, when, where and how are important. Why is unimportant. If asked, explain that it is because you said so.

I once convinced a guy who worked for me to take part in a go-kart race despite him telling me he could not drive. I told him not to be so stupid and to get his eighteen stone, six-foot-five-inch frame into the little speed machine and stop being a whinger.

It was only after the marshals furiously shepherded him back to pits with him ashen faced and trembling, following a dreadful accident, that I realised there are people who see two images independently from each other. I had always thought he had a bad squint.

$ecret Habit$ of $ucce$$ful Ba$tard$

I shudder when I think how terrifying it must have been for him to do thirty miles an hour in an unprotected seat, on a

twisted track in a dimly lit, converted bus station without being able to judge the next corner. Even though he knew the danger, he did what he did because I persuaded him to.

When you expect the unachievable, you get often get it. I once asked a very senior executive at Cisco Systems, Wim Elfrink, how our Services business was going to overcome what appeared to be an impossible goal - to increase profitability above the already world-record levels as we moved into higher risk and costlier services offerings such as people-intensive consultancy.

His reply was swift and direct, he explained to me that, "At Cisco we achieve the impossible." That was the end of the discussion and I could not really argue with him, now could I? What could I say that would intelligently challenge such a statement? It was a great lesson in what I call 'Execu-speak.'

If anyone questions your expectations, knock them back like Wim did to me. Put such doubters in their place by reminding them, helpfully, that bumble-bees should not be able to fly, that miracles happen all the time and that we are only constrained by what we believe is possible.

If they continue to complain, simply fire them and find another masochist to achieve the impossible and line your pockets in the process.

Be unreasonable

Never be pleased with anything. Whatever it is, or has been done to you, complain vigorously about it whenever you can.

Reject ideas with clenched fists. Get mad about everything.

Never miss an opportunity to complain about your job, salary, your car, your house, your last holiday, the meal you are eating, the wine you are drinking....."

If you get bored complaining about things that are under your control, start complaining about things you have little or no influence over, like the weather, the delayed train, your company or your boss, global warming..... Anyone and anything are your legitimate targets.

Elton John famously complained to Hotel staff when staying at a top London Hotel that the wind outside was too noisy. Quite what he was expecting to be done about it, God only knows.

Be bossy

When you are being bossy, raise the volume and slow the speed of your speech so that it sounds like every word has an important meaning. People will hang on your every word. People will really listen hard and even if you are talking bollocks, it will sound intelligent and interesting. Force people to listen to you. You are called 'the boss' for good reason.

Ignore all that crap about leadership, empowerment and team working. This has been written either by people who were too vain to admit that they were successful because they were tough bastards, or by people who have interviewed them and been hoodwinked.

Your life is too short to be run by a committee. You decide what needs to happen, tell people and get them to do it. Make deals happen. It is quicker and easier and if people do not like it, they are of no use to you anyway. If you have got the time and energy to spend counselling and developing people, coaching them and worrying about sharing responsibilities around, you are not spending enough time enjoying your success. Make decisions and enforce them. You may think this is being bossy. It is. That is why you are called 'the boss'.

Bossy is a word people use to describe someone telling them what they want them to do. How can anyone be successful if people do not do what the boss wants them to do? No-one really likes being told what to do, so some bosses make it look like they have allowed sub-ordinates to make decisions themselves. I recommend you bypass the pretence. Tell them what you want and when you want it done by. It is quicker and easier and you will get what you want done.

Be inflexible

Do not allow yourself to be manipulated. You manipulate others. Negotiate with people, for sure, but know your minimum acceptable position as well as your best possible. Never allow any movement below your minimum acceptable one.

I use the phrase, "That's not acceptable," a lot. No need to say any more than that. Being inflexible does not mean telling people what is acceptable. That is for you to know and them to find out.

One of my guys once negotiated a deal for 18 months with a prospective customer. 18 months!

Every week my guy would come back with another demand from the customer for more discount, added components, changes to terms. Eventually I went nuts and went to see the main man at the customer. This was a multi-million dollar deal with a major High-Street Bank and we needed it, but I had had enough of the negotiation game playing.

I met the customer executive at his offices at 08-00 on a Monday morning, 200 miles from home. Him setting the meeting for this time was a great tactic, but just added more energy to my anger. I walked in tore up the draft contract and threw it on his desk.

"The deal is off," I said, and turned to leave.

$ecret Habit$ of $ucce$$ful Ba$tard$

"You cannot be serious," he replied, "We have been working on this for 18 months."

I repeated my position, "The deal is off."

The poor guy then realises that he has pushed too far and asks me why. I tell him, "It's all in your favour and none in ours. The deal's off"

He then softens and asks why again, this time more imploring me to answer than being tough with me.

I tell him that everything he has negotiated to date is no longer OK and that I will give one concession - a discount of 25% off our list prices. He had up until that morning pushed and gained 43% discount and a host of other concessions with my guy.

He baulked a little, but then he said, "I was a bit surprised that Steve (*my guy*) gave in so often. I actually played a game with him where I wanted to see how many times I could get him to move and I was up to the Departmental record! Every time he moved, I asked him to move again, and he did."

I explained that I was not so flexible and that his game had cost us money and time. He smiled and said, "I like your style, I agree your terms and I know better now."

We closed the deal there and then with a handwritten 25% discount on one sheet of paper, rather than the 43% discount embedded in the ten page document that I had torn up earlier. It turned out to be one of our most profitable deals ever.

Learn to be inflexible. It works in your favour.

$ecret Habit$ of $ucce$$ful Ba$tard$

For study purposes, watch the senior salesperson at a car dealer that has more than 100 sparklingly clean second-hand cars on the forecourt.

Keeping others in their place

Techniques to make you ruder

"People who are smart get into MENSA. People who are really smart look around and leave." James Randi

Be abrupt

Use short, punchy, authoritative sentences. Ideally interrupt people when doing so. Raise your voice enough so that people know you are serious and when you have said what you wanted to leave, or get them to.

You can interrupt sneakily by looking at your watch whilst someone is talking to you. If they fail to spot you doing it and rush to a close, try tapping it as if to check it is still working. This is sure to make them stop talking quickly. State your point and move on.

Send very short, de-personalised e-mails. Capital letters in a bold typeface are great for getting the point across that you are, in essence, raising your voice.

If communicating by phone, use 'telephone terrorism'. Hang up when you have stated what you want done and always make sure you end the conversation.

For study purposes, watch anyone senior in the newspaper business, TV personalities who specialise in politics, the media or the arts, or anyone from Eastern Europe.

Be ignorant

When you are wealthy and powerful, you will become a celebrity and people like celebrities. People will want to be around you to share in the experience of your wonderful life. You will get people's attention whether you like it or not. Lots and lots of people will want to take some of your precious time and energy so you have no choice but to ignore lots and lots of people. You will not have the time to please everyone and now that you know this, make your life easier immediately by ignoring people from the outset. You will have to do it eventually, so start now. This is the pinnacle of ignorance.

Ignoring people is an art form worth becoming good at. Loudly yawning, or widening your eyes with the palms facing upwards are good first stages for showing no interest in what a person is saying. These can be cleverly accentuated in impact if in a group by turning to another person than the talker whilst doing them, following up with a brief half-smile.

$ecret Habit$ of $ucce$$ful Ba$tard$

The simplest form of ignoring people is to say nothing and maintain a lengthy silence after the person has finished talking. Hold an inquisitive, but otherwise blank, facial expression and wait for the reaction.

Silence is a terrific weapon. It has been used by salespeople since commerce began.

Ignoring the first objection is the first golden rule of sales. If someone objects to something, simply shut up and look at them. It creates a weird reaction in most people. Their first thought is, "My objection is so stupid that this guy is doing me a favour by ignoring it." Their next thought is that maybe they did not hear the objection, so perhaps they should repeat it. However, their brain is unable to make themselves repeat it, because of the fear that you probably did hear it and you are ignoring it for their benefit, because it is just too stupid an objection for you to respond to.

This circular problem becomes a conundrum in your opponents mind. They really should raise the objection again, but they are worried that it is so facile that you will laugh at them if they do. Sub-consciously they take the easy way out and bury the objection, usually by waffling about how unimportant it is in the big scheme of things. More silence convinces them that this is the right decision to take, so their objection is resolved.

Silence is golden. Try it when negotiating for anything, anywhere. The longer you hold your tongue, the more things go in your favour. It is amazing.

A useful technique if you find prolonged silence difficult is letting the person finish and then look puzzled and say, "Pardon me?" or "Sorry?" This usually causes the person to either repeat themselves or tell you that it wasn't really important. Either reaction will suffice initially. One further repetition of the above is usually enough to close down the subject under discussion in your favour.

Taking things a stage further, try repeating what the person has said, as if to show you have listened carefully, but get the details terribly wrong. This usually frustrates the person adequately to end the conversation after a short series of rescue attempts.

Once you have practised, there are also some advanced techniques you might like to apply. Teach yourself to look as though you are listening when someone is talking to you so that they really go to town on all the details, but then clearly demonstrate that you have not listened at all. This can be crushing. That person is unlikely to ever again bother to engage you in conversation.

By the use of regular tilts of your head, frequent raised eyebrows and the occasional, "Aha," muttered under your breath, plus a smattering of well-timed, "Yes's" and "No's," the person will believe you are listening intently and will go on much longer than usual to get the point across.

Whilst doing all this, think of anything you can that has no bearing whatsoever on what the person is talking about. This will help you make sure none of what they say sticks. For extra impact maintain a simple manual task, shuffling objects nearby, tidying up, twiddling a pen or doodling. At a suitable break, state you have not really been listening and in fact you are in a rush, say thanks, but say you have got to run.

Never look into another person's eyes. It shows that you are engaging if you do and gives others an opportunity to assess where you are coming from. The eyes are as we know a window to the soul, and a handy tip is to imagine that you would want no-one looking at yours, so do not let them.

You can manage this more easily if you focus on something on the person's face, like a mole or scar, or an aspect of their hairstyle, or in extreme cases something that is behind them. If this gets exhausting remember you can always look at your shoes. You will be branded as a tough-nut within a few seconds of dismissing eye-contact completely. It is a real winner in making opponents feel uncomfortable and it is so much easier than staring them down.

It is truly disarming to be faced with someone who focuses near your eyes, but never actually locks onto them. I know a chap who is an amazingly successful salesman who manages to always seem like he is looking at something behind you, just above your head height. Every time we meet, the urge for me reposition my head so that he was lined up properly or to turn round and check what he was looking at, was so overwhelming that I cannot remember much of what the man ever said to me, despite hours of conversation between us.

For study purposes, watch any Scandinavian entrepreneur, any successful venture capitalist, or anyone who has made so much money that they have lost interest in everything but tracking their wealth through the performance of the stock markets.

Be patronising

You can patronise a lot of things; hotels, restaurants, clubs, shops and of course people. Do so. You can also patronise charities, but I would advise against this unless it furthers your self-interest, and only once you cannot count how much money you have.

Save your special efforts for patronising people. When you patronise someone you appear to be treating them kindly but hint that they are inferior to you. After all since you know best, and you are the greatest, this should be second nature to you.

If you are in any doubt about how to patronise people, just imagine that they are a precocious teenager and you are a dominant parent.

Useful phrases are:

"If I were you…"

"In my experience…."

"With the greatest respect…."

"I am sure you realised your mistake and do not need me to point it out, but I would just like to say….."

For study purposes watch anyone in their twenties who has just got an MBA or Doctorate talking to their older and wiser boss.

Put people down

Finish people's sentences. It annoys them and gives you good practice at guessing what people are going to say.

If you are going to keep people in their place properly, ritually humiliate them in front of other people by openly criticising them for the first thing that comes into your head.

For study purposes, watch any senior manager who has made millions from share options by being in the right place at the right time, who never went to University, who reads the Sun newspaper and thinks drinking too much is an honourable pastime.

Never be polite

There is a big danger with showing people appreciation. People will think you are easily pleased and a bit of a pushover if you show them appreciation or gratitude, so resist the temptation.

Keep people on their toes waiting for appreciation and then present them something that is close to it, but is not quite there. "Thanks," is usually more than enough.

If you spend your life congratulating others and saying how much you appreciate all they have done for you, eventually they will see through this tactic and it will no longer have a positive impact on them, so do not bother.

To make this easier, get people around you who are self-motivated, thick-skinned and loyal and ditch people who need reassurance and support.

For study purposes, watch anyone who has worked for more than 10 years in a Financial Services trading environment since they left school without any qualifications or anyone who captains an unsuccessful sports team.

Confronting dissent

Techniques to make you more argumentative

"You do not have to agree with me, but it is quicker." Anon

Be abrasive

Ruffle the feathers of those around you. It helps to keep people operating at their best if you wear them down continuously. Just like when a person is hungry, they are more alert; if you oppose them gently at all times, they will be more eager to please you.

Being caustic, curt and dismissive will add just the right amount of abrasion to your relationships with others and keep them aware of their most important priority, keeping you happy.

I enjoy watching Michael Winner, the once film director famous for the 'Death Wish' films and now general raconteur and restaurant critic. Winner is the personification of abrasiveness. One actor who worked with him on Death Wish 3

$ecret Habit$ of $ucce$$ful Ba$tard$

is quoted as saying,

"The atmosphere on set was drenched in fear. [He] spent most of his time shouting at everyone, except Charles Bronson, of course. But Mr Winner was also very witty and funny, in a vicious way."

For me, Winner entered my Successful Bastards Hall of Fame when, in 2006, he was offered an OBE in the Queen's 80th Birthday Honours List for his part in campaigning for the Police Memorial Trust. He declined the honour, reminding Her Majesty hilariously that,

"An OBE is what you get if you clean the toilets well at King's Cross Station."

For study purposes speak to anyone who regularly uses a middle initial in their name, anyone with a badge that says 'Customer Services Representative,' anyone that works in IT Support and of course moody elderly film directors.

Be confrontational

If you want to be confrontational you have to quickly establish an opposing principle. Disagree on principle and do so publicly. My favourite is to simply say, "That is bollocks," after someone else has spoken.

Lord Denis Healey, the ex-Chancellor of the Exchequer with whom I had the pleasure of dining with one evening told me that he had a rubber stamp made with the word, 'Bollocks' on it that he used to stamp official reports and documents that he thought were nonsense.

If it is ok for a man that was leading the financial economy of a powerful nation to do this, it is ok for you and me too. Get your own stamp made up immediately.

For study purposes watch anyone who is over thirty years old and is still a Socialist, anyone who has been dumped by more than three lovers, anyone who files personal papers meticulously and anyone who cares what job title is written on their business card.

Turn every discussion into an argument

Arguments are competitive discussions. Knowing what you know now about the importance of competitiveness, it is obvious that we should turn every discussion into a battle to be won.

Follow the example of my dear brother Jon and start every discussion with a grimace so as to signal that before long this next chat will develop into a full blown argument.

For study purposes, watch any woman who is over 45 years old and has four or more young children, middle aged Socialists with a big mortgage or anyone who is ugly but has a wonderful body.

Make mountains out of molehills

It may not be important to them, but it is to you. Just because they think that the matter is trivial should not stop you from over-blowing the situation into a national incident.

For study purposes watch anyone with 'inspector' or 'auditor' in their job title, anyone who has given up a professional career to do full-time charity work or anyone who is unfortunate enough to be bi-polar and forgets to self-medicate.

Win every argument

An argument is a verbal competition, so you should always aim to win it.

Imagine that you are a successful barrister who cross-examines people for a living. They have some simple tricks for tripping people up. Asking the same question repeatedly but in different ways is their favourite. You simply wait for their answers to contradict one another and then you can undermine the person by highlighting the contradiction. This weakening of their position allows you to move to the 'coup-de-grace' by telling them to go away and come back when they know what they are talking about.

For study purposes watch anyone who manages a home talk to the person who earns the money to keep it running. However, if you want to understand how to win arguments without referencing things that happened 30 years ago, watch politicians at debating time or legal counsel whilst they are in Court.

Getting perfection

Techniques to make you more critical

"Honest criticism is hard to take – especially when it comes from a relative, a friend, an acquaintance or a stranger."
Franklin P Jones

Be pedantic

Being a pedant is easy. Just focus on pointless and painful levels of detail and correct everything around you that does not meet your expectations, which will be almost everything.

The joy of working at this detailed level means you will never have to look far, or for long, for things to draw people's attention to. Develop your own set of standards around the work you do that err massively towards obsessive attention to detail.

Use your natural powers of visualisation to form a view of the perfect world according to you. Make it as detailed as you can, develop and enhance it every day, so that it becomes a real and achievable world to you, then set about driving this benchmark into the world around you.

The real beauty of this approach is that everyone around you will strive to achieve the impossible – the perfection that only you can properly visualise. You will be forgiven for not operating in that way yourself, because people will realise that this is your vision, but that making the vision a reality is their job, not yours.

When you are in a position of power, you will be forgiven for not being a great detail person, but recognised as one that drives such attention in those around them. You will be described as a visionary, but not a detail person yourself – and amusingly this will endear you a greater gravitas and people will assume that because you are always grilling about them the detail, that you remember it, whereas all you will need to do is grill them skilfully.

Criticise immediately

If you fail to make your criticism immediately, you have lost an important advantage. Whenever people are criticised some time after an event, they fail to remember what it was that they actually did that upset and start to reconstruct the incident to try and rebut the criticism.

The classic scenario happens at every six-month performance appraisal that any employee has endured and relates to when they are criticised about something, a long time after the fact. They quite rightly ask, "Why was I not given the chance to repair this problem at the time. It is unfair to bring it up now, and in such vague terms."

Never delay making a criticism, because as the person making it, you leave yourself open to the standard rebuttal above. You also risk failing to remember enough of the details to make the criticism convincing and relevant. Time blurs the importance of such things, so waste none of it. Get your criticisms out at the time, immediately the event occurs.

You will be pleasantly surprised at how people will react. They will thank your for the criticism rather than resenting it. They will appreciate the error of their ways, see it with the same eyes that you have and be delighted that you are coaching them so carefully and personally.

Focus on the negative

We are built to notice the negative things, so revel in doing this. I will prove this. Ask anyone to answer the following question, "Is a button a good design?"

The answers will be something like this, "Yes, but......they come loose and fall off, they break, the hole sometimes gets too big for the button, they can be fiddly, if you lose one it can be difficult to find an exact replacement..."

$ecret Habit$ of $ucce$$ful Ba$tard$

Whoever answers will quickly find all the things wrong with the most successful clothes fastener in all of history. This is because we are pre-tuned to spot the things that are negative about something.

How many times have you heard two people talking about someone else in a positive way only? Rarely, I bet. Usually, the conversation will be peppered liberally with negative comments.

Save yourself time and forget about being positive. Focus on the negative aspects of a situation, person or thing.

There is a saying that you should wrap negative criticism in positive terms, when criticising people this is known as 'kissing them before you kick them.' I advise you to avoid the kissing bit altogether and just kick people. No-one believes you can be genuinely positive anyway, so do not disappoint them. Focusing on the negative has a much greater and longer lasting impact.

I am fascinated at how the talent shows of today have highlighted the power of negativity and brought to their 'nasty' star judges such fame and fortune. Their caustic and barbed comments are enjoyed by everyone and their nastiness is seen simply as 'honesty' by most people.

Watch Simon Cowell or Piers Morgan on any of the current talent shows, like 'The X-Factor' or 'America's Got Talent' and what you will see are men unafraid of being cruelly negative to the people auditioning before them. Similarly, Tara Banks on 'America's Next Top Model', or any of the judges on Strictly Come Dancing.

The best known and most popular judges are the ones who are most often, most negative. Why is this? Deep down we all wish we could speak our minds when we feel negatively about something and we respect people who do, because they are so rare. Focus on the negative and you will be more successful for it.

Ignore input

You know you know what is best. Make sure everyone around you knows that you know that you know what is best.

Along the way, many people will question your decisions, your approach, your strategy and your style. If they are not in your trusted inner-circle, simply ignore them. You are the boss after all.

Almost every really successful person has no advisers, except for a few people who are just like them, other self-made successful bastards. After all, if professional advisers' advice was worth taking, why would they not apply it themselves independently and achieve their own success.

Avoid consultants like the plague. They will cost you money, confuse your people and dilute what you direct others to achieve. Believe in your judgement and ignore everyone around you.

You may think that this would make people think you are

ignorant and narrow-minded. On the contrary people will see that you are committed and single-minded. Remember, that your success will be envied and applauded with equal measure, so just ignore the input of the envious and bask on the applause.

It is a technique that the most powerful businesspeople worldwide use to their advantage. Professional people have a strong sense of self-esteem and whether the unfortunate recipient or one of those.

Make your criticism personal

"'Shine a light on someone -- it's funny how numbers improve." Richard Scrushy

There is nothing as effective as making a criticism personal. The best way to achieve this is to direct it at one person, publicly, in-front a group of their peers.

It is a technique that the most powerful businesspeople worldwide use to their advantage. Professional people have a strong sense of self-esteem and whether the unfortunate recipient or one of those who look, when you deliver a direct, personal and public haranguing upon them it strikes deeply within their very souls.

It need not be even aggressive criticism. Any criticism will do, as long as it is personal. I have known of people being verbally abused publicly and even being fired for not remembering someone's name. Simply ask lots of direct questions, in rapid succession, and wait for the person to be unable to answer one - then simply criticise the person by name, very directly and imply that if they cannot manage to answer such a simple question, how can he or she be expected to run their part of the business, this project, that branch, this team..........

You may think that this would make people hate you, but bizarrely the opposite is true. You will be seen as someone who drives others to perform at their absolute best. People will love you for your direct approach and your courage when confronting weak and underperforming people.

Building a fear culture

Techniques to make you more aggressive

"When you have them by the balls, their hearts and minds will follow." Jerry Martin

Be loud

Boom your instructions and orders. Never be afraid to raise your voice. Shouting at people is a remarkably powerful weapon. It is disarming to the people around you and reduces the chance of that person, or anyone within earshot, ever incurring your displeasure again.

Reserve your best and loudest outbursts for solving the toughest problems and for dealing with the most obstinate people. Develop the capability to be loud, without being angry. Control your anger and just raise your voice to a deafening volume. You can practice this in private first, in front of a mirror. Loudness without the normally associated anger is doubly disarming. Most people receive the message immediately and sub-consciously they will accede to your demands immediately, fearing that the next level of your wrath, being loudness AND anger, is something that must be avoided at all costs.

The very best exponents at this technique are theatre directors and Shakespearean actors who have to project their voices to be heard. For study purposes watch the actor Brian Blessed.

Be abusive

There is nothing like an expletive or two, aimed at a person directly, to make them upset. Swear frequently and crudely. It adds a dimension of menace to what you say. Some very successful bastards have made a foul mouth part of their trademark and are not thought of any the worse for it.

Take the most successful British chef in history for instance, Gordon Ramsay. This gutsy 40 year old ex-professional footballer is the only chef in London honoured with three stars by the Guide Michelin and he has developed a celebrity greater than any of his competitors and a wealth to match.

He is best known for liberally using the word 'fuck,' and its derivatives, more than anyone who has ever been in the public eye. He even had a TV series broadcast called 'The F Word.'

He loves abusing people, including his colleagues and competitors alike. He called his ex-boss Marco-Pierre White, to whom he says he owes "everything," a "fat bastard" at his own wedding. Of Ainsley Harriot another celebrity chef he said, "Ainsley's not a chef, he is a fucking comedian." He is also happy to criticise nationally loved personalities, such as legendary Australian talkback radio host John Laws: "That John Laws. What a knob. What a fucking knob."

When opening his first restaurant in New York City, a New York Times reporter witnessed him spotting a waiter with a tie that had a knot broad enough to bring Ramsay's abusive fury down upon him:

"Young man, what's your name?"

"Swapon, chef."

"Your knot, it's very big, don't you think?"

"Yes, chef."

"You know what they say in Britain—the bigger the knot, the smaller the cock. Young man, I'm sure your cock is very big. Will you do something about your knot, please?"

"Yes, chef."

Be bad-tempered

If you wander around with a smile on your face all the time, you will look oily and complacent. Look miserable, threatening and bad-tempered instead.

If you behave in a bad-tempered way, people will avoid you. That is good. It means you will spend less effort on time-wasters with pointless ideas and having to deal with stupid people with stupid problems. Only the really important things will come to your attention.

I used to work for a guy in Banking who was well-known for being bad-tempered in the morning and drunk in the afternoon. You had a choice if you wanted to get a decision from him. Face a bollocking in the morning or listen to a load of bollocks in the afternoon. This meant that wherever possible, you avoided any contact with him whatsoever and just got on with your job. This left the old successful bastard plenty of time in the mornings to recover from his hangover and freed up his afternoons to get slaughtered drunk all-over again.

For study purposes watch elderly policemen who are still in uniform, middle-managers with problems at home, anyone with a drink or drug problem or anyone suffering from an invisible, but critical, illness.

If you wander around with a smile on your face all the time, you will look oily and complacent. Look miserable, threatening and bad-tempered instead.

Do not ever give people compliments. It builds their strength and saps yours. Be insulting instead. It keeps people on their toes.

For study purposes, watch anyone with an honorary title, anyone who farms a lot of land or anyone who has inherited an enormous amount of money. If these are unavailable simply watch anyone who does not have 'a pot to piss in' but still manages to find the money to drink heavily every day.

Be physical

Verbal assault is one thing, but nothing beats getting physical with people when it comes to making an impressive impact. It does not have to be totally over the top and into 'Grievous Bodily Harm' territory, even though as we know the punishment 'knee-capping' punishments used in Ireland by some of their organised thugs have deterred many young villains from a criminal path.

Your physical presence alone can be adequately threatening and you can use the power of a very firm handshake or robust pat on the back to establish your position beautifully. If you struggle to intimidate people by touching them firmly, simply throw things at them or gently cuff them around the head.

If you are all-powerful, everyone else must be weak. Therefore, do not feel embarrassed or awkward about bullying the weak, because it includes everyone on the planet near enough. They deserve it and it will help them build stronger characters for themselves. Survival of the fittest has been a pretty successful model to date.

Speak to anyone who was bullied at school in later life and they will tell you all the positive things they got from the experience. It made them tougher, made them stand-up for themselves and made them into the strong person they are today.

For study purposes watch anyone greet another where either one has played a contact sport, was once in the Armed Forces or has studied martial arts to avoid being bullied and failed to grasp the spiritual side of it. To perfect the art of throwing things at people, watch any woman having a row at home with their partner after he has been caught doing something she objects to deeply.

Be explosive

When you get upset, do not sulk and walk off. Make a scene by having a violent tantrum. When people have so obviously upset you despite your best efforts to instruct them in how to behave there is nothing better than to bring them back into line by throwing a monumental wobbler.

I have seen some exceptional Executive tantrums, from smashing fists down on desks to boardroom chairs and projection equipment being thrown around meeting rooms. Performance is disastrous, *bang*, forecasts have dropped, *crash*; everyone in this team will be fired, *smash*. Add your purple face of rage and the uncontrolled salivation of madness and I can tell you it makes a definite and lasting impression on anyone on the receiving end.

The most wonderful tantrum I have heard of is one thrown by Tom Siebel of the eponymous Siebel Corporation, a giant application software company, who met an ex-executive of his Dr. Steve Garnett, in the reception area of a San Francisco hotel by chance.

Dr. Garnett had recently left Siebel's employ after pocketing a few tens of millions of dollars from stock options and had joined a competitive start-up called SalesForce.com. Being one of the few likeable successful guys in the business, Garnett had subsequently been followed there by other key Siebel employees.

Siebel, having assumed that Dr. Garnett was wilfully poaching his staff, was so apoplectic with rage towards him that, as he came down a sweeping staircase to the lobby flanked by his bodyguards, he unleashed a torrent of angst upon him.

Tom was out of control and shouted across the lobby, "Hey, you know what you get when you moon a Gorilla?" Steve had little clue what Tom was talking about at first, but he did not have to wait long to hear the answer. At the top of his voice Tom screamed, "You get fucked up the asssssss!"

Explosive grandiose behaviour is a key component of the successful bastard's kitbag and throwing a major tantrum is a great way to show how serious you are about something. Let rip and enjoy.

Incidentally, having sold his company to Oracle Corporation, Tom has retired peacefully to southern Florida. Having got away from his employees now, it has been reported that he now satisfies himself by persecuting those people tasked with making his retirement a comfortable one, like his personal trainer.

I am sure you will agree that if it is acceptable for CEO's of giant publicly owned corporations to throw very public and explosive tantrums, it is OK for you to as well.

Never give up – Being Ruthless

"It is a very funny thing about life; if you refuse to accept anything but the best, you very often get it." William Somerset Maugham

Be fearless	Harness your fear	Be powerful	Lead from the front	Fear no-one	Ignore pain
Be incisive	Be direct	Be precise	Be focussed	Be decisive	Be quick-witted
Be determined	Be tenacious	Be persistent	Be driven	Be committed	Be disciplined
Be unforgiving	Blame everyone but yourself	Never allow an appeal	Write people off	Publicise others' failure	Never forget
Be cruel	Be spiteful	Slander people	Spread vicious rumours	Bully the weak	Punish severely

Bringing out the warrior in you

Techniques to make you fearless

"Let me not pray to be sheltered from dangers but to be fearless in facing them. Let me not beg for the stilling of my pain, but for the heart to conquer it. Let me not look for allies in life's battlefield but to my own strength. Let me not cave in."
Rabindranath Tagore

Harness your fear

Use fear to your advantage. Most people are frightened of lots of things and many of these are irrational fears. Phobias like fear of heights and open spaces and common fears like of public speaking or raising complaints in public are irrational, yet many people suffer with them. Do not allow yourself to be weak like them. Fear nothing.

The best way to destroy any fears you do have is to force yourself to confront them. Do this whenever the opportunity arises and see it through. Such conditioning will, over a short period of time, build your defences to the point that nothing will bother you. You will have turned your fear to your advantage - turned fear into an opportunity for greater success.

Be powerful

Power is energy divided by time. The higher the energy level and the shorter the time it is applied, the greater the power. Keep your energy levels high. Get a reputation for being a driver, a mover and a shaker. You will live your life at high speed so the apparent power you have will be huge.

They say that knowledge is power. This is because it takes energy to turn information into knowledge, so if you can have knowledge instantaneously that would have taken much time to acquire, that knowledge has great power invested in it. It is potentially the most important thing you can have.

Physical power is useful, if you possess it and at the very least you must appear to be strong to others. Never accept that you have any weaknesses and push yourself forward on your strengths, whatever they are.

Lead from the front

Set the right example of leadership and demonstrating what you want by leading from the front. Imagine yourself as a military commander in days of old. Not like one of those hapless First World War Generals, sitting in headquarters quaffing alcohol and toasting muffins on an open fire, but get back to the Roman times, when Barbarians and the Roman legions alike were led by warriors.

With luck, once you have led from the front once or twice people will get the picture and you can go back to relaxing and enjoying the spoils from the labour of others, but you must first set the standard for others to aspire to.

I worked with a wonderful guy, Andrew Skehel, also known since as 'Swampy,' who put leading from the front down in history one day. Our team of workers were on an 'outward bound' team building experience one night, dressed like soldiers and indulging in an orientation exercise.

In the dead of night we had to traverse from point A to point B through dense woodland and gather instructions for the next leg of the mission. Andrew's leadership was outstanding, not least because of being Sandhurst Military Academy trained and a driven guy. He decided, against almost everyone's view, that we should travel in a certain direction and he led us that way, from the front of course.

Our troop proceeded to walk through the dense wood and

despite us wading through some significant puddles of water; he was adamant that we should continue to advance. Not one to be dissuaded easily, he led his team of ten or so people into deeper and deeper water within this wood. Despite my suggestions that, as we passed a small rowing boat entangled in the thick undergrowth, we might be heading the wrong way, he pressed on. It was only when the shorter members of our troop were struggling to keep their heads above water, and our Special Forces 'guide' was getting concerned that his chest high waders were about to be breached, that 'General' Skehel realised that he was in fact walking his team into an icy lake that had burst its banks and encroached into the wood.

I will never forget that night and I learned a great deal. People will follow idiots happily into hazardous conditions, against their better judgement and even if they know the leader is wrong, if their leader appears confident, vocal and determined. Why will they do this? They will do this to avoid a difficult confrontation with the leader and because they do not believe in themselves strongly enough to take a stand.

If you have the choice, which you do, be the leader, not the follower. At least if you get cold and wet in the process, it will be your own doing not because someone senior to you was being obstinate to the point of lunacy.

Fear no-one

I have never backed down from confrontation and neither should you. In my experience pain is relative to your belief in your own invincibility. Go in hard and you will not get hurt. I like to remind myself that everyone has to shit, even the important people. It provides an endearingly powerful image when you realise that everyone is built the same way as you.

Everyone is insecure, concerned about their inadequacies and fearful of something more powerful than themselves. Successful bastards just hide it better than others.

If you show no signs of weakness and never back-down, the lowliest David can beat the biggest and baddest Goliath.

Ignore pain

Pain comes in two different forms - physical pain and mental anguish. We all feel pain and some of us are good at managing it and others struggle to do so. You need to develop a thick enough skin to ignore pain, whatever its form.

$ecret Habit$ of $ucce$$ful Ba$tard$

You are unlikely to get much physical pain, unless your chosen profession is martial or heavily manual, so I will concentrate on pain that is caused by mental anguish.

You should teach yourself to be de-sensitised to the suffering of others, much in the same way that any doctor has to. You also need to apply this same level of attention towards your own ability to deal with the painful challenges you will face. You have to be strong, powerful and forceful and to back that up with strong defences.

Never allow yourself to be ill. It is bad for business. I know that with the power of positive thinking and a sensible approach to living, your body can handle phenomenal pressures without breaking down. The day you decide that it is all too much, that you just cannot stand it any more, that you worry about what other people think of you, and so on, will be the day your defences come crashing down. Your immune system will collapse and you will become ill. On the other had, ignore pain, stay positive, refuse to give in to illness and you will stay strong and healthy.

Building energy and creating action

Techniques to make you more incisive

"Along with a strong belief in your own inner voice, you also need laser-like focus combined with unwavering determination."
Larry Flynt

Be direct

The biggest mistake anyone can make is to approach a situation in a round-about way. Be direct and concise. When you speak, make only the most salient points as single stand-alone, direct messages.

If you ask a question, make it probing and direct, but open enough to strike fear into whoever has to respond. Never let them off with a simple yes or no answer.

Waffle and piffle are pointless. Get to the point and leave no ambiguity in what you say.

Be precise

If you are direct, you are half-way already to being precise. Make sure that the facts you use are clear and correct and unambiguous.

This will mean, naturally, that you will say less and the content of your communication will have a greater impact. When you communicate people will listen.

If you do not know the answer or having nothing of substance to add, avoid bullshit, just keep quiet. Precision must become a way of life for you.

Be focussed

Focus on only those things that hold your interest, where you can add value and that will improve your personal position in life. Make sure you know what these things are. When you are focussed you are formidable and people will come to realise that if you want something, you will achieve it.

Avoid distractions and people that enjoy distraction. Concentrate on completing and finishing things, not leaving them hanging. Review your performance at the end of each day and make sure that you have achieved a focused conclusion to key tasks.

Be decisive

Decisions are the most important things in anyone's life. Think for a moment about how many really important decisions you have ever made. Think about the ones you stuck with to the bitter end. These will be the ones that have served you best.

Replicate the behaviour you applied when making and following through on these key decisions and apply the same rigour to ALL your decisions.

Decisiveness is one of the most powerful and attractive characteristics that you can display as you build your fortune. Most people are fearful of making decisions, change their minds without good reason and give up when the going gets tough. Most people are not successful bastards and this is one of the main reasons why. They fail to make any decisions forcefully, they do so irregularly and their decision can never be seen as 'final.'

Do not fall into this trap. Be decisive.

Be quick-witted

It is not the big that east the small, it is the fast that eats the slow. Those who do so with a smile on their face are the most valuable people on earth. If you can keep smiling during a tense situation, and manage risk and adversity with humour and grace, you will be seen as a person of power and someone to be both feared and admired.

Sharpen your wits and hone your sense of humour by making sure that you appreciate the humour that underlies every human situation. Develop your senses about others, about how they feel in a particular situation and how they react and use this to your advantage. Be quick to act, above all.

For study purposes, watch, the TV show, "Have I Got News for You." One of my favourite lines ever on that programme came from Michael Winner in December 2005, when asked to comment on pictures from the recent news he was shown a picture of the Buncefield Oil Depot Fire and exclaimed:

"Ah, that must be George Best's cremation"

197

Keeping the faith

Techniques to make you more determined

"Some succeed because they were destined to, but most succeed because they were determined to." Anon

Be tenacious

Tenacity is an important attribute and means that you will never let go. You will hold every opportunity you pursue until it concludes to your satisfaction.

Maintain a vice-like grip on the things that are precious to you – people, possessions, ideas, information. Ownership brings great responsibility and you must keep what you own safe and secure.

To demonstrate your tenacity, let it manifest itself, as I have mentioned before, in a ridiculously powerful and over-extended handshake. If you couple a fixed and riveting stare into the other person's eyes while shaking hands, they will realise immediately that you are a person that will not let go without a fight.

My friend and colleague, Hans Otterling, a former High School champion wrestler turned serial entrepreneur and investor, has the firmest handshake I have ever been on the receiving end of. It is a fearsome, gut-wrenching experience and imparts more than 1,000 words about him and they are all big ones.

Get yourself some springy hand clasps, so that you can build your handshake to be like his or if you are young, take up wrestling.

Be persistent

"I have not failed. I have just found 10,000 ways that will not work." Thomas Edison

The most famous example of persistency is that of Thomas Edison. He just simply would never give up and his quote above that relates to his multiple experiments to create an electric light bulb, is just the most apt to support the message I want you to receive.

I want you to die happy in the knowledge that you gave everything you did, everything you had. Imagine the satisfaction that this will bring. A life lived well, to the full, complete and full of real achievement.

<u>Be driven</u>

In my experience, whenever somebody is in your circle and combines hard work with an intelligent application and overcomes all obstacles along the way, they are described as driven. You need to be driven to succeed - obviously, clearly and continuously.

If people call you driven, you will have achieved your aim. Your determination will shine through and influence everyone around you to overcome all the hurdles before them.

Be committed

"Genius is one percent inspiration, ninety-nine percent perspiration." Thomas Edison

Here is a dilemma. You want to be committed and work hard to achieve your aims, but at the same time be lazy and have loads of leisure time. This might seem like an insoluble conundrum, but it is not. Simply be committed to things that other people deliver for you.

Leverage your opportunities by setting the framework of action and objectives and then get the others to deliver. You may have to work intensively for short periods at the beginning, but the bulk of the work will be delivered by others, so this should not be too painful for you.

As Franklin D. Roosevelt once said:

"When you come to the end of your rope, tie a knot and hang on."

Be disciplined

"It's easy to have faith in yourself and have discipline when you're a winner, when you're number one. What you've got to have is faith and discipline when you're not yet a winner."
Vince Lombardi

I have found that discipline is one of the critical ingredients in life, but one that is malleable to you. One person's discipline is another's disorganisation. You will need to discipline yourself to your own standards.

The trick that will change your life is to make sure that you do things every day. The cumulative effect of daily practice is dramatic and stunning. I practice martial arts and meditation daily, not intensively, but I do it every day. The power that this builds within me is quite awesome and allows me to perform what would appear to impossible feats of strength and destruction. There is an energy inside you that will be unleashed with daily practice of whatever you do. If you write well, do it daily, if you sing well do it daily, if you pick good stocks or horses, do it daily. You will, I guarantee, be stunned at the ways in which your skills improve with daily practice, even with minimal efforts.

Do yourself the favour of your lifetime and be more disciplined, doing what you enjoy and do best, every day.

Creating a blame culture

Techniques to make you more unforgiving

"It is a purely relative matter where one draws the plimsoll-line of condemnation, and if you find the whole of humanity falls below it you have simply made a mistake and drawn it too high. And are probably below it yourself." Frances Partridge

Blame everyone but yourself

Look for scapegoats at the first sign of failure. Look for people who can be blamed. These people are everywhere. They will usually be the ones that look up to you, operate obediently and faithfully, and have their noses wedged firmly up your backside - the 'Yes Men.'

The beauty of blaming 'Yes Men' is that when you ask them if it was their fault, they will usually say, "Yes," just to please you.

$ecret Habit$ of $ucce$$ful Ba$tard$

Do not waste time criticising people's behaviour, performance or work. It is them you should criticise, not their actions. The world is full of wannabe, no-hopers who fail to take responsibility for their own behaviour, performance or quality of work.

Do not bother to waste your time wrapping things in cotton wool when criticising someone. Some people say you should kiss them before you kick them and kiss them before they leave. You should just leave out the kissing altogether. Starting, sustaining and ending with a negative has a much greater impact.

In a job I had many years ago, my team were responsible for developing and implementing a complex computer system for a major UK Bank. Their IT Director was one hell of a successful bastard when it came to managing suppliers. Nothing was ever good enough and we had to bend over backwards to just keep this guy off our case.

Every one of our monthly review meetings would open with this guy saying, "I was disappointed ...." And he would then follow up with negative criticism of all and sundry. It was so awful, that to amuse ourselves we used to count the number of times he would say the word 'disappointed' and measure our success on that value, relative to the value gained at the last meeting.

After a few such meetings we decided to turn the tables and my guy managing the project and I came up with the aim of saying the word first, before he could, and then saying it more times than he did during the meeting itself.

We would open the meeting by saying how disappointed we were that his personal assistant was unwell and how disappointed we were that the coffee machine appeared to be out of order, or that the train was late, or the lift took ages to arrive. It was all we could do to keep ourselves from breaking down in hysterics when his usual reply was something like , "Forget about being disappointed about the coffee machine, I am disappointed that you failed to deliver the last software release on Tuesday evening as planned…."

It did not have much impact on the meeting, or his volume of criticism, but it was great fun and that is more important, especially during tough times.

For study purposes watch any American manager carry out a performance appraisal of one their staff or any successful bastard that is employing you on a contract to do work that his people are incapable of doing themselves.

Never allow an appeal

For people that you have blamed, there is never any need for them to apologise. No excuses are necessary, because none will be accepted. Have such a sign made up for the wall in your office to make sure everyone realises this.

Your decision is final. The buck stops with you, there is no room for any appeal, so do not entertain one. Your natural powerful and decisive nature will be clear enough to anyone early on, so they will accept their fate honourably in all likelihood.

Learn to block out the word, "Sorry," should anyone be foolish enough to use it. Of course they are bloody sorry, so they should be. They should have thought about that before they did whatever they did.

For study purposes simply watch any judge in a region of the world that orders the death penalty for drug traffickers

Write people off

No excuses or apologies should ever be accepted, no appeals entertained, and not just now - forever. Dismiss the people from your life that fail you and move on.

You should not worry about this. There will be many other people, better people, who will want to share in your success and try even harder than the last to please you, so waste no time in writing people off permanently if they fail.

For study purposes, watch a Head Teacher and how they deal with a highly intelligent, but rude and disruptive, teenage pupil.

Publicise others' failure

Criticism for failure, whilst directed personally, should be delivered publicly.

My favourite example of making failure public is the ritual dealt out to Cantor Fitzgerald traders in London who had the weakest performance over a week's trading. For the following week they were made to wear, or when seated, hang on the back of their chair, a blazer with just a W and an anchor embroidered on the back. How wonderful is that?

For study purposes, watch employees at any trading firm in a financial capital or read any tabloid newspaper on a Sunday.

Never forget

Be like my wife, Hilary. She never forgets. Like many women she can remember my transgressions of 30 years ago with a vividness that shocks.

She cannot seem to remember any of the good things I have done, but then why should she? She wants to keep me on my toes, after all.

Handing down punishment

Techniques to make you crueller

"Cruelty would be delicious if one could only find some sort of cruelty that did not really hurt." *George Bernard Shaw*

Be spiteful

If you want to be cruel, you must start by developing a passion for being spiteful. It is the root of cruelty.

You must develop the skill to be able to be nasty and vindictive towards people that upset you, picking on their most sensitive characteristics and chastising them for that.

Look at people and sense their immediate weaknesses and shortcomings. Zoom in on these and make frequent reference to them.

One of my colleagues, many years ago nicknamed me 'Gobby' because I had delivered a master class in conversational shouting when managing a gorge-crossing exercise on an outward bound team building course. He showed a total mastery of finding an innocuous characteristic about someone and then blowing it up to larger than life size, through an appropriate nickname

It was a powerful way to warp an apparently friendly gesture and deliver it in such a way that it was spiteful, reasserting his superiority over me in the process every time he used it, which was very frequently and very publicly. I love the guy by the way and he is still a personal friend, but Andrew Skehel, you are and always will be a spiteful rascal.

Slander people

There is nothing like the opportunity of a bit of corridor tittle-tattle to destroy someone's reputation. When I operated at the top of business, I tried never to leave a meeting whilst it was in progress, because that would be the cue for the boss and everyone else to slander me. Same thing with conference calls. If you do not believe me, stay on the next conference call after you have been instructed to leave it, usually while the boss then talks to a the top tier of managers and assistants. Put your phone on 'mute' setting and listen in. I guarantee that you will learn more than you think if you get the chance to do this.

How did I know that such things would happen after I had left the meeting or call? Simple; it happened when anyone else left and I had remained, so the chances were that I would not be treated any differently.

$ecret Habit$ of $ucce$$ful Ba$tard$

There is no need to get paranoid about such things. They are a fact of life. Just get busy slandering everyone else and hope that the degree and volume you dish out outweighs that which is aimed at you.

Spread vicious rumours

"A rumour is one thing that gets thicker rather than thinner as it spread." Richard Armour.

I have usually found that rumours I have heard turn out to be true. As my dear late maternal Grandmother, Hilda, used to say, "There's no smoke without fire."

She applied this to anyone that she had a sneaking suspicion of being responsible for anything she disapproved of, which was just about everything. In reality, most people feel this way. If there is a hint of something untoward about someone, it is probably true.

Being a successful bastard is all about seizing opportunity and winning against the competition that will inevitably pursue you. You want to beat all others to the prize. If you choose to unfairly undermine your opponents in the process, all the better - and there is no better way to undermine people than to spread vicious rumours about them.

It is effortless to start or simply pass on a vicious rumour about someone. The grapevine and gossip network will do the rest for you. You can just sit back and wait.

Pick a subject that is very difficult to prove or disprove to taint you opponents with. If it is difficult or near impossible to prove or disprove it, it can be as distasteful and unbelievable as you like.

Question your opponents' mental health, sexual orientation or penchant for illegal narcotics. No-one will ever question you for hard evidence, if they do, say simply that someone close to them told you.

I have been aware of people being accused of early-morning drinking, fiddling expenses, skiving on the golf course to the extremes of having their had genitals pierced, suffering from hard-drug addiction, being active in the 'swinging' scene, having paedophiliac tendencies and even practicing bestiality with their pets. On every occasion I have assumed these vile things to be untrue, yet a part of me has said, "Hmmm, maybe, just maybe…."

It is in our nature to believe the worst about people. Nothing makes for a more exciting conversation than one laced with salacious gossip.

For study purposes, watch any group of people who meet regularly on the occasion that one person does not show up, or simply stand in a corridor, a rest-room or a smoking area and just keep your ears pricked up.

Bully the weak

One nice thing about being all-powerful and super-successful is that by definition everyone else is weak by comparison. Bullying the weak is just the same as bullying anyone around you.

If you want to get on in this life, you have to be prepared to bully people. You can call this 'using your powers of persuasion,' 'leadership,' 'direction,' whatever. Make it sound as palatable as you like, but you will need to be a bully to get what you want done.

If people find your bullying offensive, that's fine, they are supposed to. Treat them mean, to keep them keen. The weakest people around you will wilt under the pressure. Whether they were on your side or not, it does not matter because both groups deserve your wrath. Weak people need to be bullied out of your way.

I worked with a delightful guy called Erik Tiller, a successful Norwegian venture capitalist who had some fantastic ways to bully those around him. The fact that he was stocky to the point of being as wide as he was tall, helped to give him that menacing edge.

Erik's favourite bullying technique was to ask you where you were every time he spoke to you on your mobile telephone. It had a curiously painful impact on you when on the receiving end. It implied that he wanted you to realise that you were not to have any fun whilst working for him. "Where are you?" would trigger deep anxiety in the receiver, and make that person squirm to explain how busy they were working for him. It was never easy taking such calls on the golf-course, no matter how properly business related the round of golf was.

I remember Erik bullying one of his top CEO's and eventually firing him for underperformance. He came into my office afterwards and proudly proclaimed that this was the thirtieth time he had fired a CEO of one of his companies. I remember thinking at the time how bizarre it was that Erik saw this as something to be proud of and then afterwards, on reflection, realising that this was one way that successful bastards measure their power and influence – how many senior people they have discarded on their way.

When you become self-made you will need to operate like Erik. People need to be worried about what you are capable of and that you will not hesitate to hurt them in some way if you do not perform to their fullest satisfaction. You need to have left a lot of people in your wake.

Punish severely

Most people appreciate that punishment is good for them. They expect it and benefit from it. I had the pleasure of surviving a Catholic school run by the De La Salle Brotherhood, which seemed to me to be a club where deviant sadists and pederasts got to act out there fantasies on children.

Corporal punishment was good for me. It built my resilience to pain and sharpened my competitive skills. For many years consecutively, I topped the table of people who had been struck by teachers most often. I even racked up a maximum score in more than one school week by receiving the maximum punishment, 'getting six' as it was known, each and every day.

I love the story of Sir Kerry Packer, the late Australian billionaire media mogul and son of Sir Frank Packer, when he was a schoolboy and came home from boarding school for his holiday minus his tennis racket which he had forgotten. Sir Frank, being a man to instil serious discipline in his sons, immediately sent him back to school to get it.

That in itself is perhaps not surprising, but the trip from home to school, being from Geelong to Sydney, was a 1,200-mile journey. Kerry telegraphed his father later, "Arrived Melbourne safely, no love, Kerry." Delightful.

Take your punishment with grace and dish it out with zeal. It makes for a much richer life experience.

Keep everyone guessing – Being Unpredictable

"Being on the tightrope is living; everything else is waiting."
Karl Wallenda

Be enigmatic	Be complicated	Be secretive	Be eccentric	Embrace change	Be independent
Be deceptive	Manipulate people	Be two-faced	Confuse people	Be charming	Cheat at everything
Be unreliable	Be insincere	Be imprecise	Fail to keep promises	Tell big lies	Live a lie
Be dishonest	Evade tax	Be corrupt	Cook the books	Steal everything	Spy on everyone
Be reckless	Take big risks	Live life on the edge	Move at high speed	Abuse your power	Endanger others

Creating mystery

Techniques to make you more enigmatic

"I have come to believe that the whole world is an enigma, a harmless enigma that is made terrible by our own mad attempt to interpret it as though it had an underlying truth."
Umberto Eco

Be complicated

The best way to keep people guessing is to be complicated in your behaviour. Develop hidden depths. Swing your moods and change your preferences, re-invent yourself every few years and try not to do the same thing too often.

Think of the most colourful and interesting people you know. They will have varied tastes and a style that is difficult to imitate. You never quite know what they will do next. They are unpredictable and enjoy variety.

Develop multiple and what might appear conflicting interests and hobbies. Invest your time and money in many different projects. Diversify your exposure to people, associating with

216

people from all walks of life and levels of society. Gain pleasure from many things, have an eclectic taste for music and reading. Get the tabloids and the broadsheets, read 'get rich quick' books and Karl Marx.

Keep moving, changing and re-directing what you do. At the very least you will confuse the opposition; at best you will be able to take any stance honourably when it suits you.

Be secretive

Secrecy is a requirement for humankind to survive. Certain information must be kept secret to keep society in order, keep people comfortably in their place. All governments keep secrets, all employers keep secrets and all individuals keep secrets. They have to.

Imagine a government that had no secrets. What would an opposing government or terrorist force do with such information? Clearly, they would use it against their 'enemy' to further their own aims. We would not want Osama Bin Laden knowing the locations, procedures and launch codes for our nuclear weapons arsenal, now would we? If it was well known how to get into the vaults of the Central Bank, how long do you think the nation's money would be safe there?

$ecret Habit$ of $ucce$$ful Ba$tard$

If the long term strategies for major companies were well known, where would their competitive edge be derived from? What is everyone in a firm knew exactly what everyone else earned? What if the designs of everything ever made were common knowledge, how would one product ever be differentiated from another? Why would anyone invest in building anything new and revolutionary, if the intellectual property were immediately shared with everyone?

We need secrecy, all of us, at every level of our lives. Find me two people who live together who have never held a secret from one another, and I will be surprised. We all have some deep, dark secrets that no-one knows.

As a successful bastard, secrecy is your weapon. You do not want anyone knowing what you think, what you are planning or how you intend to behave in the future.

Be like the Barclay brothers, Sir David and Sir Frederick. The secretive, some might say reclusive, businessmen who own the Ritz Hotel in London, several newspapers and magazines, including the Telegraph and The Spectator and their flagship retail empire, Littlewoods. The twins are famous for avoiding publicity and live on their own island Brecqhou, one of the Channel Islands, located just west of Sark. In 2007, their estimated their wealth was £1.8 billion.

These painters and decorators turned mega-businessmen rarely give interviews and operate their companies through complex off-shore companies, financial trusts and investment vehicles.

Be eccentric

I am not proposing you get quite as eccentric as say, David Icke. I would not recommend believing and then writing that there are a race of reptilian humanoids known as the Babylonian Brotherhood that lead world events and that many prominent figures are reptilian, including George H W Bush, HRH Queen Elizabeth II, Kris Kristofferson and Boxcar Willie. Bless him, but David Icke is clearly mentally ill.

You need to be eccentric more like old Judges, very wealthy business-people and landed gentry are. Develop a passion for things that are a little bizarre. Collect weird things, follow obscure sports and maintain a belief or two that make people's hair curl when they find out. Live in a Hotel permanently, like so many famous people have before you. Insist on wearing a particular item of clothing that stands out unusually, regardless of the occasion. Be a little bit Howard Hughes.

For study purposes, watch anyone with a triple-barrelled surname or that insists people use their middle initial when introducing them to others.

Embrace change

"I shall adopt new views so fast as they shall appear to be true views." Abraham Lincoln

No-one likes change, but in our modern world, change is part of daily life. Adapting to what is happening around you is essential to your survival and without it you cannot prosper.

The greatest fortunes have been made by people who exploited major changes in the world. Mining, oil, steel, railroads, cotton, tobacco, tea, cars, newspapers, plastics, drugs, media, technology, telecommunications, bio-technology and most recently the Internet have all been the root of personal fortune for many. Jump on the new industries and exploit them before others do.

If you have a clue about what is coming next, invest money and time in it. Those people that spotted the Internet early and were lucky enough to invest in Google, the search engine at flotation in August 2004, for example will have seen a $100 investment grow to over $600 today. If you had invested the same amount in Cisco Systems, the telecommunications giant in 1990, it would be worth more than $53,000 in 2007 and all without you having lifted a finger to help.

"It is not the strongest of the species that survive, nor the most intelligent, but the one most responsive to change."
Charles Darwin

Be independent

"Familiarity breeds contempt." **Aesop**

If you follow the crowd you will simply end up an indistinguishable part of it. That is not your aim. You want to be different. You want to be part of that exclusive club of successful bastards. You may think this group could itself be called a crowd and if you visit Bermuda or Monaco, Manhattan or Knightsbridge, you might get a glimpse of the crowd, but believe me they are a group of individuals and not a crowd. They will have made individual fortunes in unique ways and operate lives that are anything but those lived as one of the masses.

Be a trend-setter, have your own views and maintain an independence from those around you. You are special and people need to realise that. Use your independence as a beacon to show your uniqueness.

Using your cloak and dagger

Techniques to make you more deceptive

"A little inaccuracy sometimes saves a lot of explanation."
HH Munro

Manipulate people

Change your style to meet the needs of a situation. Manipulate people to your way of thinking, by adapting yourself to synchronise with what they want to see.

Watch Gordon Brown, or any politician for that matter, as he or she travels around the country, and see how they change the way they speak depending on the region that is being visited or the group that is being addressed. If you have no time for politicians, watch any state appointed defence barrister when talking to someone with no qualifications, no family and no job.

Be two-faced

Being duplicitous or two-faced is a necessary evil. If you are a CEO you have the shareholders and the employees. You cannot treat both groups of people the same way. You have to have more than one face.

If you have children, the old saying, "Do as I say, not as I do," applies. Would you be happy letting your child smoke at the age of seven, even when you know you did yourself. No; of course not. You have to have multiple faces, not just two. We all do.

Since we know everyone is two-faced or worse, why not exploit that to your advantage. Put the face on that suits the person you are with.

For study purposes, listen to anyone from Glasgow talking to another Glaswegian, then listen to them talking to their English spouse. One will be an unintelligible monologue of grunts and the other a rhythmical rendition like that of an 'old-school' English television newsreader.

Confuse people

The fundamental art of deception is based on confusing people. You need to move them to a place where they are unable to anticipate what is going to happen next. You need to wrong-foot people and keep them off balance, the way a professional football player can wrong-foot a defender simply by looking one way and going another.

Be charming

What is it that makes us think someone is charming? I believe it is one thing above all that makes someone appear charming. They genuinely listen to you. What better way to charm someone than let them talk about themselves and appear to be genuinely interested in what they say.

The challenge for you is to work out who to be charming with and who you need not bother with. You can make your own decisions, but I recommend you be charming to anyone you live with, your mother and anyone you are selling something to. You can be as nasty as you like to everyone else.

For study purposes watch anyone that is trying to get you into bed or sell you something that you do not need. Maybe you can do both at the same time?

Cheat at everything

As was mentioned earlier, even Carl Lewis, the vocal anti-doping multiple gold medallist sprinter, took performance enhancing drugs. He cheated, was found out and got away with it. Over the counter herbal cold medicine was to blame apparently.

The positive results occurred at the Olympic Trials in July 1988 where athletes were required to declare on the drug-testing forms "over-the-counter medication, prescription drugs and any other substances you have taken by mouth, injection or by suppository," which Mr Lewis failed to do.

In 2003, Dr. Wade Exum, the United States Olympic Committee's director of drug control administration from 1991 to 2000, gave copies of documents to Sports Illustrated that detailed 100 American athletes who failed drug tests and should have been prevented from competing in the Olympics, but were nevertheless cleared to compete. Among those athletes was Carl Lewis.

It was revealed that Lewis tested positive *three* times before the 1988 Olympics in Seoul, Korea for pseudoephedrine, ephedrine, and phenylpropanolamine which were banned stimulants. Lewis was then banned from that Olympics and from any other competition for six months. Subsequently, The US Olympic Committee accepted his claim of inadvertent use and overturned the decision.

"Carl did nothing wrong. There was never intent. He was never told, you violated the rules," said Martin D. Singer, Lewis' lawyer, who also said that Lewis had inadvertently taken the banned stimulants in an over-the-counter herbal remedy.

"The only thing I can say is I think it's unfortunate what Wade Exum is trying to do," said Lewis. "I don't know what people are trying to make out of nothing because everyone was treated the same, so what are we talking about? I don't get it."

I think it all the more amusing that in the 100 metres final at the Seoul Olympics, Ben Johnson, the Canadian sprinter won Gold and set a new world record. However, Johnson was subsequently stripped of his World Record and of his gold medal, both of which were handed to second place Lewis instead, when Johnson tested positive for performance enhancing drugs. Johnson's records have been erased from history, while Lewis's remain.

Letting people down

Techniques to make you less reliable

"Figures do not lie, but liars figure."   Oscar Wilde

Be insincere

"It is dangerous to be sincere, unless you are also stupid."
George Bernard Shaw

If you can fake sincerity, you can fake anything. Master this skill.

For study purposes, watch HRH Queen Elizabeth when meeting a member of the public or a politician talking to a member of the great unwashed - the unemployed.

                   www.successful-bastards.com

<u>Be imprecise</u>

Follow the example set by all the world's politicians. Develop the ability to not answer questions, but still give animated and compelling responses.

The trick is to always know what you want to say and say that. If you do not like the question, simply prefix what you would like to say with phrases like:

"It's more a case of......

"You have missed the most important point, which is….."

"The problem has less to do with <reference the question> than it has to do with ……."

If all else fails, "I am not at liberty to comment at this time," usually works wonders.

For study purposes, watch any sub-committee of any Government, anywhere, investigating an important suspected breach of public trust.

Fail to keep promises

Do not worry about quality, delivering on time, delivering to specification or meeting commitments. Get other people to worry about that stuff for you.

For study purposes read any political party's manifesto and compare it to what is delivered after a few years in office.

Tell big lies

"It is better to be quotable than to be honest." **Tom Stoppard**

Tell lies a lot. Tell a lot of lies. The nice thing about lying is that most people believe you. It is human nature.

Do you know anyone who has never told a lie? No? Neither do I. We all lie. We have to lie. Just watch the film "Liar, Liar," starring Jim Carrey, if you do not believe me.

The nice thing about lying is that most people believe you. It is human nature. Little white lies, all the time. A story embellished, a detail changed, an honest opinion not expressed to avoid upsetting a loved one. We are programmed to lie and

$ecret Habit$ of $ucce$$ful Ba$tard$

most of us are pretty damned good at it.

The little lies are OK, big lies are great. When people believe them it can have a major impact in your favour. Lie at will and tell big lies. No-one will mind. It will be just another of your skills that people secretly admire.

I have worked with many professionals who lie routinely and still hold their jobs down very successfully. Advisors who lie about their knowledge, lawyers who lie about what they know and do not know. I know managers who lie about what is going to happen or not to their employees, company owners who lie about their plans and company results, Presidents and Prime Ministers who lie about matters of State, senior policemen who lie under oath. I am sure you do as well.

Sometimes, we all have to lie, even tell really big lies. Self-preservation and the desire to improve our own position force us to lie. There is no need to feel ashamed about telling big lies. On the contrary, you should exploit the opportunity and just do what every other successful bastard does, and do it better than them.

For study purposes watch anyone in an important and trusted position who is under threat and wait for their lips to move.

Live a lie

People will be fascinated to discover that you are an International canoe instructor, black-belted martial artist in more than one style, an accomplished musician, a painter and scientist, one-time Junior Wimbledon champion and Falklands war veteran.

Maybe you think that is a hard list of accomplishments to pretend you have, but let me tell you that a professional colleague of mine, who was thirty-two years of age in 1992, claimed all this at that time and got away with it, despite having had 15 years work experience in Information Technology companies. I hope that Ian Clarke is still thriving.

The more complex and confusing the falsehoods you create about yourself, the less likely anyone will be able to fathom the truth from the fiction.

OK you went to Oxford to study English, even though that was evening classes in Creative Writing at the Oxford School of Creative Writing, but you still went to Oxford to study English. If a member of the House of Lords can get away with this, so can you. Bless you Lord Jeffrey Archer.

If you want study practice, read any unauthorised biography of anyone in the public eye.

Cooking the books

Techniques to make you more dishonest

"Behind every great fortune there is a crime."   **Honore de Balzac**

<u>Evade tax</u>

"Good people do not need laws to tell them to act responsibly, while bad people will always find a way round the laws."
Plato (427-3487BC)

   Only two things in life are certain, death and taxes. Not true, death maybe, taxes most definitely not.

   Almost every country's taxation system looks favourably on those who purport to create wealth for others. Some look so favourably on the wealthy that they become tax-havens for the obscenely rich and powerful. Monaco, the Channel Islands, the Cayman Islands, Bermuda....

$ecret Habit$ of $ucce$$ful Ba$tard$

According to research published by the Tax Justice Network in 2005, the estimated wealth 'openly' held in tax havens is costing governments around the world up to US$255 billion annually in lost tax revenues. This does not include corporate tax 'hidden' there, so the number is substantially higher in reality.

To put this in perspective, US $255 billion annually could provide adequate health services for every person in the world or permanently eradicate world poverty within six years. It is quite simply a staggering amount of money.

You should not therefore worry about evading tax yourself. Your impact on the world will be small in comparison and the benefits to you will be great.

Whether you stay in your native country, or become a tax exile, when you have a lot of money you will pay less tax than the average person.

In the UK for instance, if you can afford to leave money in your company for four years you only pay 10% tax, instead of the usual 40%. Imagine that you earn £1m a year, which many successful bastards do. That means you will be nearly £6,000 per week better off for burying your money in your company and then extracting it just a few years later. Forget Pay As You Earn, go self-employed and start your own company.

I remember reading about that successful bastard Mohammed Al Fayed, owner of Harrods, the Paris Ritz and Fulham Football Club to name just three of his flagship enterprises. Until recently, Al Fayed had an 'agreement' with the Inland Revenue as a resident in the UK that he would pay £250,000 income tax each year and they would not investigate his earnings further. That means that he was assessed as if he was earning around the equivalent of £650,000 annually if paying at 40% or at worst £2.5 million if paying at 10%. With what this guy owns and the lifestyle he supports he just has to be earning 10-100 times that, but because of his 'arrangement' he is evading tax within the law.

Be like Mo. Make an arrangement with the tax authorities if you like the country you are living in. They know that if they do not agree, you will simply hide it all from them anyway in some labyrinth of off-shore financial trusts and holding companies, or just move somewhere else that is more kind towards you.

If you have to relocate, I recommend Monaco, where income tax is a pleasing 0%, but you can only get in if you can show a £1M or so in the Bank beforehand, so get busy earning it now.

$ecret Habit$ of $ucce$$ful Ba$tard$

<u>Top Ten Most Corrupt Heads of State</u>

Name	Position	Funds embezzled
1. Mohamed Suharto	President of Indonesia (1967–98)	$15–35 Bn
2. Ferdinand Marcos	President of the Philippines (1972–86)	$5–10 Bn
3. Mobutu Sese Seko	President of Zaire (1965–97)	$5 Bn
4. Sani Abacha	President of Nigeria (1993–98)	$2–5 Bn
5. Slobodan Milosevic	President of Serbia (1989–2000)	$1 Bn
6. Jean-Claude Duvalier	President of Haiti (1971–86)	$300–800 M
7. Alberto Fujimori	President of Peru (1990–2000)	$600 M
8. Pavlo Lazarenko	Prime Minister of Ukraine (1996–97)	$114–200 M
9. Arnoldo Alemán	President of Nicaragua (1997–2002)	$100 M
10. Joseph Estrada	President of the Philippines ('98–2001)	$78–80 M

Source: Transparency International Global Corruption Report 2004.

Be corrupt

"No-one can earn a million dollars honestly." **William Jennings Bryan (1860-1925)**

You may not be lucky enough to be a Head of State and relieve your country of a chunk of its national wealth like the successful bastards in the top ten table, because these guys are at the pinnacle of their game and they each are more of a bastard than you ever need to be, but it is comforting to know that so much is available to people who are corrupt.

You do not have to be at the top of things to benefit. Even lowly Congressmen in the United States have great opportunities to line their pockets.

In late 2005, the watchdog organisation Citizens for Responsibility and Ethics in Washington published a report alleging that 13 members of Congress, including senior representatives, had violated a variety of congressional ethics rules.

It must be said that everyone named below denied any wrongdoing, but their alleged transgressions, whether true or unfounded, make a useful aide-memoir for anyone in power wishing to feather their own nests.

• Sen. Bill Frist: The report accuses him of violating federal campaign finance laws in how he disclosed a campaign loan. It also calls for an inquiry over his recent sale of stock in HCA Inc., his family's hospital corporation. The sale has raised questions about possible insider dealing.

• Rep. Roy Blunt: The report criticizes him for trying to insert provisions into bills that would have benefited, in one case, a client of his lobbyist son and in another case, the employer of his lobbyist girlfriend, now his wife.

• Sen. Conrad Burns: The report says that questions arose over $3 million in appropriations he earmarked for an Indian tribe in Michigan and associated substantial campaign contributions.

• Rep. Bob Ney: The report says the chairman of the House Administration Committee went on a golf outing to Scotland in 2002, arranged by a lobbyist at a time when the congressman was trying to insert a provision into legislation to benefit one of the lobbyist's clients.

• Rep. Tom Feeney: The report says he incorrectly reported that a golf trip to Scotland 2003 was paid for by the National Center for Public Policy Research, which denied it. A Feeney aide said the congressman had been misled. Questions also have arisen about two other privately funded trips.

• Rep. Richard W. Pombo: He paid his wife and brother $357,325 in campaign funds in the last four years, the report says. He also supported the wind-power industry before the Department of Interior without disclosing that his parents received hundreds of thousands of dollars in royalties from wind-power turbines on their ranch.

$ecret Habit$ of $ucce$$ful Ba$tard$

- Rep. Maxine Waters: The report cites a December 2004 Los Angeles Times investigation disclosing how members of the congresswoman's family have made more than $1 million in the last eight years by doing business with companies, candidates and causes that Waters has helped.

- Sen. Rick Santorum: The report says he encountered controversy over disclosures that Pennsylvania taxpayers paid for his children's schooling while they lived in Virginia.

- Rep. Randy "Duke" Cunningham faces questions over his dealings with a defence contractor who allegedly overpaid him when he purchased Cunningham's house.

- Rep. William J. Jefferson is under scrutiny for his role in an overseas business deal.

- Rep. Charles H. Taylor: The report says that questions have been raised about his private business interests, including a savings and loan in Asheville, N.C., and personal business interests in Russia.

- Rep. Marilyn N. Musgrave: The report accuses her of misusing her congressional office for campaign purposes.

- Rep. Rick Renzi: The report accuses him of financing portions of his 2002 campaign with improper loans.

If you are lucky enough to lead a major corporation the opportunities to act in a corrupt manner are endless.

In 1999, F. Hoffmann-La Roche Ltd., currently the sixth largest pharmaceutical company in the world, pleaded guilty and agreed to pay a record $500 million fine, and BASF pleaded guilty and agreed to pay a $225 million fine, for leading a worldwide conspiracy to fix, raise and maintain prices, rig bids for contracts and allocate market shares for vitamin products.

Cook the books

There are so many cases of companies cooking the books and individuals at the top of the company benefiting from the fraud that hundreds of books have been written about them. And these are just the cases we know about. Here are three of the best, in summary.

In 1996, Daiwa Bank pleaded guilty to multiple felonies and paid a $340 million criminal fine, the largest ever at that time, for covering up massive securities trading losses on two separate occasions and deceiving and defrauding bank regulators.

In December 2001, the energy giant Enron filed for the then biggest bankruptcy in U.S. history. Enron's collapse resulted in 20,000 employees losing their jobs and many of those also lost their life savings, having been encouraged by their CEO, Kenneth Lay to buy stock at a time he was dumping his.  Investors worldwide also lost billions.

$ecret Habit$ of $ucce$$ful Ba$tard$

Lay, who earned $42.4 million in 1999 and had sold more than $300 million of Enron stock options since 1989, was brought to trial found guilty on ten counts of criminal conspiracy and fraud, and for making false financial statements. His sentencing was scheduled to take in October 2006 and he faced up to 20 years in prison for his crimes. However, he died of a heart attack at his home in Aspen, Colorado on July 5, 2006, before sentencing could be carried out. He subsequently had his conviction 'vacated' which despite many protests mean that his record is not formally blemished.

During his trial, Lay claimed that Enron stock had made up about 90 percent of his wealth, and that his net worth in 2006 was a negative $250,000, which just goes to prove that even if you have no money there is no reason why you cannot own a holiday home in Aspen.

On July 21, 2002, one of the largest telecommunications in the world, WorldCom filed for Chapter 11 bankruptcy protection, at the time the largest such filing in US history. WorldCom's audit department had uncovered a $3.8 billion fraud in June 2002, during a routine examination of company accounts. This later turned out to be more like $11 billion.

From 1999 through May 2002, the company had, under the direction of Bernie Ebbers (CEO), Scott Sullivan (CFO), David Myers (Controller) and Buford Yates (Director of General Accounting) used fraudulent accounting methods to make its declining financial condition look instead like growth and increasing profitability by under-reporting costs and failing to expense them properly. Their auditors were the now defunct and discredited, Arthur Andersen who had been dissolved following the collapse of Enron.

Bernie Ebbers, made some spectacular personal gains from WorldCom before he was found out and brought to justice. At his peak in early 1999, Ebbers was worth an estimated $1.4 billion. His personal holdings included ownership of Canada's biggest ranch, which was bigger than Wales, several farms, timber forests and lumber companies, a yacht builder, nine hotels, a trucking company and a hockey team. All of these businesses were funded by his WorldCom stock and during 2001 as WorldCom stock plummeted, Bernie Ebbers persuaded WorldCom's board of directors to provide him corporate loans and guarantees of over $400 million to cover problems he had servicing this debt.

However, Bernie got bashed up badly for being a naughty boy. On 6 September 2006, he was sentenced to 25-years in prison. He now languishes in low-security incarceration at Oakdale Federal Correctional Institution in Oakdale, Louisiana having driven himself there in his Mercedes. The earliest date he will be considered for parole is 2028 when he will be 85 years old.

Bernie did the right thing by all accounts and gave back all his ill-gotten gains and is now said to be worth less than $50,000. He famously said during his trial before taking the Fifth Amendment, "I know what I don't know. I don't know technology and engineering. I don't know accounting." Which does make one wonder how he became the chief executive of a Telecommunications company?

If all you know is how to be a cowboy, do not let that affect your confidence when applying to be a global corporate leader.

Just make sure you don't spend all your time on the ranch.

Steal everything

Most people do not have original thoughts and are not creative. Most people are too swept up in the daily shit-storm of life to lift their heads out and think of something new. If they do, the chances are it will come to nothing and be lost amongst everyday distractions. Most new ideas are adapted from old ones. Changed a little maybe, but stolen all the same.

Most people assume that Hoover invented the vacuum cleaner, but it was a chap called Hubert Cecil Booth who invented the machine in 1900.

Like so many inventions, it was copied and adapted from someone else's idea. Booth had watched a demonstration on a train at St Pancras station of a device aimed at replacing the dustpan and broom. This device blew dust into a container. By all accounts the demonstration was an abject failure, but it sparked an idea in Booth's head – why not suck it up, rather than blow it around? Booth went home and placed a damp cloth over the arm of his chair and using his mouth and lungs literally sucked through the cloth and on seeing the results, his idea for the vacuum cleaner was born. Within one year, Booth had built and patented his first vacuum cleaner, which he called the Puffing Billy, a massive machine that had to be carried on a horse-drawn cart.

Spy on everyone

If you are not able to know something that no-one else knows, simply know something that non-one else knows you know by spying on them.

There have been many cases publicised about spying, mainly where one government spies on another. There are multiple government agencies openly accountable for organising spying. It must come as no surprise to you that spying is an every day fact of life.

It has been reported that the UK's Government Communications Head Quarters (GCHQ) 'listens' to every conversation made by phone and reads every e-mail sent or received in the UK and automatically scans them for potential threats and criminal activity.

Ask any drug dealer or career criminal you know how many phones they use and how often they change them, if you do not believe me.

Taking and sharing risks

Techniques to make you more dangerous

"Playing safe is only playing"   Chuck Olson

Take big risks

"When choosing between two evils, I always like to try the one I have never tried before."   Mae West

If you do not like risk, do not bother getting up in the morning. Stay in bed, you will be safe there. If you decide to get up and go out, then embrace risk at every turn. The trick is not to be risk averse, but be risk aware.

Develop risk mitigation strategies for each venture that presents itself. Always have a contingency plan, be prepared for things to go wrong and know what to say and do before the bad things happen.

Once you are comfortable with taking risks, take even bigger ones. Push the envelope on it. Big risk, well managed, delivers big returns.

Live life on the edge

"Attention to health is life's greatest hindrance." **Plato**

Stress is good for you. Stress is a normal experience. The word stress was first coined in relation to human beings in 1935, before that it was only ever used by engineers.

Be a fatalist, you are going to die for sure sometime. Better to live a day as lion than a lifetime as a sheep. You are here for a good time, not for a long time. Your life will pass you by in an instant; do not waste time worrying about the consequences of your actions. Just get on with it.

Ignore all the risks and go for it, go large. What is the worst thing that can happen? You will experience the thrill of life and may die in the process, but what a way to go. When you rest, rest well, but make the most of your body and your opportunity to experience pleasure for the rest of the time.

Over the years, there have been so many scaremongering warnings about everything, including every food you can think of, including meat, sugar, butter, eggs and fats; most things pleasurable, including alcohol, smoking, narcotics, rock music and sex; most things in everyday use, including microwave ovens, aerosol cans, computer screens, mobile phones, cars; and for every possible lifestyle, including inactivity, jogging, working hard, playing sports ...... The list is truly endless.

Ignore it all. Worrying about it will add an unnecessary and pointless burden to your life. If you smoke, smoke. If you enjoy over-eating, indulge. Death has its eye on you regardless and with all the possible ways you can die, who knows which one it will be.

When you are wealthy and powerful you can survive things that would kill ordinary people thanks to the investment you will make in keeping yourself alive using artificial means. Use your wealth to provide yourself that extra chance over the masses.

If you enjoy narcotics like Keith Richard of the Rolling Stones, why not detoxify yourself a few times every year with a total blood transfusion, or like Rod Stewart, have regular MRI scans to detect even the minutest change in the health of your vital organs. Get yourself a fully staffed medical team at home like Hugh Hefner, of Playboy fame. You can afford to live life right on the edge and you deserve the opportunity.

Move at high speed

"If it feels like you are in control, you are not going fast enough." *Mario Andretti*

It is not the big that eats the small. It is the fast that eats the slow. Get your self, your idea, your product or your company moving fastest in its market. Focus on the opportunity, make the decision and then execute swiftly.

If you do things quickly you will have first mover advantages, you will be able to cream off the best return from taking the higher risk.

Abuse your power

Power corrupts and absolute power corrupts absolutely as we know. When you are powerful, you will not be able to help yourself. You will abuse your power. It may start at first with some funny practical jokes to amuse yourself and move onto full scale abuse of those around you. You will not be able to resist. It is as certain as that night follows day that you will abuse your power, so you might as well do it consciously.

What is the point of having power if with it come no advantages? The two things are inseparably linked. In fact, the definition of power itself includes a built in authority to abuse and exploit others. Do not be shy about this; just get on with enjoying it.

Endanger others

You are important to your self and to those around you. So, if you have the option, endanger others before endangering yourself.

Take enormous risks, ideally with other people's money and energy because yours is more precious than theirs. Create a culture where people will follow you over the cliff, or ideally jump off without you, if you say so. It will make their lives more exciting and fulfilling and ironically they will be grateful for it or at the least reluctantly accept that it was their fault for agreeing to it.

Work the people around you mercilessly hard and expect the impossible from them in terms of work rate and output. Make it clear that their health is not your concern. The most important thing is to get the job done. Disregard safety rules when it suits you and the job needs to be done by the crazy deadline you have set.

$ecret Habit$ of $ucce$$ful Ba$tard$

When is the last time you heard of a 'four-star' General being killed in action? Never right? Does that tell you anything? If not, go back to page one and read this book again. Get real.

How to avoid going too far

To do, or not to do, that is the question?

You have now had the opportunity to read, learn and think about 100 ways to be more of a bastard. Some will have curdled your blood and churned your guts. Some will seem totally inappropriate for you to ever be able to deliver. Some will have made you laugh heartily. Some will have seemed great, common sense based ideas that you practised immediately.

Herein lays your biggest challenge and most important question? To do, or not to do? I have said that this book will stir up your thinking of how to approach the world that it will challenge your core beliefs and I hope it has. Now it is time to reconstruct them in a better way - one that will make you more wealthy, successful and happy.

So, when should you apply which techniques? Sadly, I cannot help but to tell you to go your way. Plough your own furrow and make these habits, traits and techniques suit you. You decide here, not me.

I recommend you review each set of 25 techniques, habit by habit, and ask yourself some searching questions. How could these things help me be more successful? Can I carry them off? When should I apply them? Use recent real-life experience to

support the way you feel when making this assessment. Live
through the scenarios you remember and visualise how you
could have had an improved outcome from a past failure,
imagine how you might address an upcoming challenge more
effectively.

One thing I guarantee is that even if you fail to apply a single
one of the techniques, ever, you will see them clearly in the
future when they are being used against you and will be better
prepared to react to them, happy in the knowledge that this just
another example of a successful bastard applying a simple
technique to get what they want from you. With luck, you will
be able to smile and take it. I do hope, however, that with some
application you will be able to counter it with your own.

Imagine that your boss is a successful bastard. For most of
you, this will be easy because they are. Imagine what their
reaction will be if you use some of the techniques on them. Will
you get fired, or will you slowly chip away at their veneer of
nasty behaviour, penetrating it long enough for them to realise
that you are in fact a formidable opponent and not one of the
down-trodden masses. I bet you that you will pierce their
armour and no matter how momentarily, this will register. Soon
you will see a pleasant change happen. In meetings your boss
will spend more time making eye contact with you than others.
Key tasks will be passed your way. Your opinion will be sought
more often and you will be able to have more influence on what
is going on around you. Keep working and ideally get the boss
out of the way and become one yourself. Your aim is to have no
bosses, so start making those plans now.

Every time you feel weakened, refresh your mind by scanning

the techniques. Visit my web site and see that you, like millions of others, can make a really positive difference to your lives by just being that little bit more self-centred, tough, ruthless and unpredictable.

When to ease off

You can be and will be tough, but as everyone knows, you may meet clearly tougher opposition. So the next big question is when do you ease off?

I like to ease off just before someone threatens suicide or appears to want to kill me. There are not that many emotional reactions in-between that I worry about. You may think that I am joking here, but I promise you I have seen both ends of the spectrum more than once in very real, very clear and stark relief.

My message is, if you are tough enough ease off just before someone dies.

At another more practical level, you should ease off when the risk of an action or outcome outweighs the potential reward. No point in banging your head against a brick wall as they say. Know when things are looking dead as ducks and be prepared to ease off. I would also recommend that with children, very close friends and immediate family, you ease off all the time. There is no need to make everyone's life miserable.

Managing the common risks

What is the worst thing that could happen to you? You could die, right? What are the next worst thing and the one after that? Take some time to think of these and you will come up with the something like the following:

1. I might die

2. My health might be adversely affected

3. I might go to prison

4. My family may be hurt

5. I might be unable to do what I want

6. My spouse might leave me

7. I might lose all my savings

8. I might lose my job

9. I might lose my means of earning a living…..

$ecret Habit$ of $ucce$$ful Ba$tard$

Have a look at your list now and consider one 'worst thing' against another. Have you really got them in the right order? Do you really know what is important to you? I bet not. Change them around now.

Keep your list of risks front of mind and weigh up every opportunity, every decision you make against them. You will be amazed that almost none of your decisions come anywhere near being related to any of the 'worst things.' What does this mean? It mean that we can massively change our positions in life without even having to take any real risks at all, at least none that would have an outcome in the 'worst' category.

Use this technique to manage risks associated with all projects and endeavours, write them up, weigh them up and keep them in view. When the risks appear to be becoming more likely and you need to work out whether you should take the risk, simply write up the rewards in the same way, starting with the best and working your way down.

1. I might become world-famous

2. I might make some really useful and influential friends

3. I might make a ridiculous amount of money

4. I might open up exciting and new opportunity

5. I might learn something valuable

6. I could make people happy

7. I might secure a useful income stream

8. I might be able to give my job up and be my own boss

9. I might gain something from the experience…..

Use these simple lists to compare the relative merits and weights and make your decisions based on the way you feel.

Remember that your feelings are either 'based' in your head, your heart or your gut, or some combination of all three. The ones in your head are the logical or imaginative ones, the ones in your heart relate to your core beliefs and the ones in your gut relate to your innermost fears and doubts. If one part of your thinking engine is overpowering another consciously shift your attention to one of the other thought centres and balance the feeling.

If you are in any doubt still about what to do, concentrate purely on your heart, imagine warmth around it and think hard what your heart is telling you. It is the most powerful thought centre in your body and knows best. Believe me, try it. It works.

Taking out the best 'insurance policies'

All successful people use contingency plan and have an exit strategy from any endeavour that they are involved in. They are prepared to change tack, adapt to a new way and if necessary even bail out.

Insure your success by making sure that you know what to do in advance by planning what might go wrong and what you would do about it. They say that the person is someone who has done it successfully before. You will have, albeit only in your mind, but the power of imagination and visualisation will allow you to foresee problems and overcome them immediately they arise.

Whatever your thing, your business venture, project or ambition, think it through in advance in the greatest detail to the point where you have actually 'lived it.' All the great entrepreneurs do this, so should you.

If the risks outweigh the rewards, it is time to bail out. You have not failed - just pick up on one of the other projects you have running.

Things to avoid doing too often

You need to be prepared to operate a variety of the techniques in this book and not overuse any of them. Changing the way you behave and adapting to the situation at hand will be key skills and the best way to develop these is to practice variety in your life.

I would suggest you try to avoid criminal action too often. It is too risky. Try not to get involved in businesses associated with organised crime. The fact that these people are organised is what should alert you to the risks. If they are organised and fear no consequences of their actions at all, they will be an opponent too formidable for most of us. Besides, who wants to end up propping up a motorway, or rotting in a prison cell for life?

If you find that behaviour backfires when you practise it, try once or twice more, but if it fails, it may be best to put it to one side for use in emergencies only. Sometime, no matter how hard you try, you are just not made to do some of these things. That is OK. We all have a few weaknesses. Even if you find 10 techniques impossible, you still have 90 more to choose from.

Avoid the crime if you cannot do the time

The whole world of business, law and government is so tightly interwoven that the chances of anyone in the legal or political system really wanting to punish one of their 'own' is low. The potential of them one day being found out and having to face the same punishment you do will sub-consciously scare them from making an example of you. However, the risk is very real that if you do get found out you may be punished.

You can therefore assume that for every successful bastard out there, a 'fall from grace' moment awaits them. If they are good at it, they might never be found out. That is your aim. Never get caught. However, it may not be easy.

Every day the papers tell us of some successful bastard that went too far off. This is usually the only time we know the truth behind their success. Until a successful person's name is highlighted in this way, they are getting away with it.

Often, it says that whatever was going on, usually of a serious and criminal nature, had been going on for years. Years, during which that person got away with it.

If you are unlucky enough to be caught, tried and convicted, slim though that chance is, you will be able to look forward to lenient punishment, comfortable 'open' prison conditions that will be more like a school dormitory than a prison and an opportunity to hold onto your ill-gotten gains for you to enjoy on your release.

White-collar crime is never punished as severely as other crimes, so try to make your fortune in this way, rather by purely criminal means.

259

What to do if it all goes horribly wrong

There are several tactics to mitigate the disaster of it all going horribly wrong. I have put these in the order that you should consider them:

(1)   Maintain your innocence

(2)   Run away and hide

(3)   Develop a serious illness

(4)   Get religion

(5)   Take it on the chin, do your time and start again

(6)   Top yourself in mysterious circumstances.

$ecret Habit$ of $ucce$$ful Ba$tard$

Maintain your innocence

When Richard Scrushy, the chief executive (CEO) and founder of HealthSouth, a US-based global healthcare company, was fired in 2003 after being implicated in a $1.4Bn fraud where, in certain fiscal years, the company's income was found to be overstated by as much as 4,700 percent, he resolutely maintained his innocence. Despite five executives, including two Chief Financial Officers (CFO's), pleading guilty to criminal charges of overstating profits for many years, Scrushy refused to roll over. Suspicions had first arisen in late 2002, when Scrushy sold $75 million in HealthSouth stock several days before the company posted a large loss.

Scrushy certainly lived the high life, with his wife Lesley, taking more than $200M in profits from share transactions since founding the company to fund their lavish lifestyle, with four homes, including a mansion in a Birmingham suburb not far from the company's headquarters, and a $3 million lakefront house at Lake Martin, a 92-foot yacht, "Chez Soiree," and more than 35 cars, including two Rolls-Royces and a Lamborghini. When the company crashed in 2003, the share price dropped to just cents and millions lost their life-savings.

Scrushy was the first CEO, and the only one to-date, to be tried under the Sarbanes-Oxley Act for the fraud that occurred at HealthSouth. On June 28, 2005, the jury in Birmingham, Alabama found him not guilty. He was acquitted on all of the 36 counts that were brought against him. A member of the jury was quoted as saying, "The lack of evidence is what produced the verdict."

Even if you are the founder of a failed business, use your hypnotic charm to win people over, including a jury should it be required. Just because you appeared to be the most detail conscious, controlling and involved leader, it does not mean that you knew everyone around you was cooking the books for years.

Bear in mind that maintaining your innocence might not save you if you are pursued with a persistent vengeance by the authorities. Poor Mr Scrushy was unlucky in that respect and was eventually convicted in June 2006, on bribery charges.

Four months after his acquittal, he was convicted of arranging $500,000 in campaign donations in exchange for a seat on a state hospital regulatory board and sentenced to 82 months in prison, given three years probation and ordered to pay $417,000 in fines and restitution. He was also ordered to perform 500 hours of community service. Hardly a severe punishment for a man who had gained so much?

When we remember major fraudsters, we should remember that it is not just men who are guilty. In 2002, Martha Stewart, the world famous businesswoman took out full page newspaper adverts to proclaim her innocence of securities fraud one day after quitting as the chief executive of the retail empire that she ran. She protested that, "I want you to know that I am innocent and I will fight to clear my name." You will read more about Martha later.

Run away and hide

My favourite example of recent times is Saddam Hussein, who despite encouraging everyone in his close circle to fight to the death, actually ran away and hid in a hole in the ground. Not a recommended strategy if you are a head of state under siege by unforgiving Americans, but in Saddam's case he only had one other option really and he was clearly too cowardly to take that route.

Other world leaders have done a great job running away to avoid their punishment. Many other disgraced heads of state have managed to run away and hide in exile after being offered safe-haven in other countries.

Idi Amin – Uganda – to Jeddah, Saudi Arabia

Ferdinand Marcos – Honolulu, Hawaii

Jean Claude Duvalier – Haiti - to Paris, France.

If you are not lucky enough to be a head of state, but are more a run of the mill criminal, find a place in the world where there is no extradition treaty with your home country. It worked well for many years for German criminals in South America, British criminals on the Costa Del Sol and American criminals in Mexico. You will no doubt find a big gang of like minded people when you get there, so this should reduce the level of home-sickness you suffer.

Who knows, if you have enough money you might be able to

buy your own island and declare it your own independent nation.

Develop a serious illness

No-one, bar the most ardent sadist, likes to punish someone who is unwell. If you are looking for a bit of leniency, try faking a serious illness.

My favourite example of a guilty person developing a serious illness to reduce their punishment is the case of Ernest Saunders, the former CEO of Guinness plc (now Diageo) who is by all accounts the only person to have ever recovered from the incurably fatal Alzheimer's Disease.

'Deadly' Ernest, as he was nicknamed by the staff at Guinness plc in recognition of his ruthless cost-cutting initiatives was a man who was prepared to bend the rules and early in 1986 he indulged in some highly irregular practices, including what the DTI described at the time to include providing, "unjustifiable favours for friends and himself," that resulted in an artificial boost to the Guinness share price, which in turn made the takeover of another company, United Distillers, more likely to succeed.

In August 1990, Deadly Ernest was charged and convicted of conspiracy to contravene parts of the Prevention of Fraud (Investments) Act 1958, false accounting and theft. Along with famous business leaders at the time, Sir Jack Lyons, Anthony

$ecret Habit$ of $ucce$$ful Ba$tard$

Parnes and Sir Gerald Ronson, he had conspired to buy Guinness shares to boost the share price. The scam was uncovered when Ivan Boesky, the corrupt junk bond trader, was investigated and it transpired that Saunders had passed $100M to Boesky to invest in the company. Saunders was sentenced to five years in prison.

Saunders appealed against his sentence and in May 1991, his sentence was reduced to two and a half years because Lord Justice Neill said that he was satisfied that Saunders was suffering from Alzheimer's Disease which is, as we all know, an incurable and ultimately fatal disease. With full parole taken into account, Saunders was then released from Ford Open Prison on 28 June 1991 having served only 10 months of his sentence.

After his release, Mr Saunders 'miraculously' recovered. In an interview with The Times published in January 1992, Saunders said the symptoms were a result of a "cocktail of tranquilisers and sleeping tablets" that he had been prescribed, and that he was making a good recovery.

Since his release and subsequent recovery, Saunders has worked as a business consultant for mobile phone retailer Carphone Warehouse and the investment company Seed International, and been chairman of the executive committee of a petrol credit-card company, Harpur-Gelco.

$ecret Habit$ of $ucce$$ful Ba$tard$

Take it on the chin, do your time and start again

Martha Stewart, having denied any impropriety initially, voluntarily stepped down as CEO and Chairwoman of her own company and went on trial in January 2004. She was found guilty in March 2004 of conspiracy, obstruction of an agency proceeding, and making false statements. She was sentenced in July 2004 to serve five months in jail.

Stewart began serving a five-month prison term while her appeal was still pending in October 2004, at Alderson Federal Prison Camp in West Virginia. She was released on March 4, 2005, after which she was placed under home confinement and required to wear an ankle bracelet for an additional 5 months.

According to U.S. Securities and Exchange Commission allegations, Stewart avoided a loss of $45,673 by selling all 3,928 shares of her ImClone stock, the day before the stock value fell 16% as a failed drug announcement was made public.

Martha's business is now back up and running and she is recovering her position as the most loved American housewife and homebuilder.

There is not enough room here to list all the successful bastards that have done prison time. There are just too many. However, there are many Lords and Ladies, Right Honourables, Knights of the Realm, Captains of Industry and pillars of the community that are serving, or have served time behind bars.

Being caught, convicted and sentenced to a prison term should not put you off in any way. Simply bounce back; having marked the experience down as character building and one that is closed once it is completed. Besides, you will still have all that money to enjoy spending after your release. Whilst you are incarcerated you will be treated well and have an opportunity to brush up on all those things that you had little time for on the outside.

Write a book about it even and make some money. Most successful bastards do.

Get religion

We already saw that Richard Scrushy got punished in the end, but that has not stopped him from continuing to profess his religious beliefs. He and his wife Leslie still run their own religious 'mission' and if you look on-line at their web-site *http://www.richardmscrushy.com/* you too can feel as amused as I was when you read that:

"Richard and Leslie have been leaders in the Birmingham community for many years and have a strong desire to see the community grow and prosper. The purpose of Viewpoint is to be a forum in which the spiritual leaders of our community and nation can teach God's word and discuss His truths. Viewpoint is a place where Biblical truth and theology can be discussed freely and openly, spreading the Good News.

"The guests on Viewpoint range from local bishops and

pastors to nationally and internationally known spiritual leaders. It is Richard and Leslie's desire that God's name be glorified in our community"

I have always been fascinated at how irreligious people suddenly discover God in times of great hardship or conflict. Most people reserve this switch for when their death looms before them, but successful bastards will often console themselves with the absolution that becoming religious provides when they are caught out.

My favourite 'getting God' example is that of Jonathan Aitken, the former UK Government Minister who was caught out when he lied under oath about receiving gifts from a Lebanese businessman acting on behalf of the Saudi's, whilst acting at the top of government, in his defence during a libel case against the Guardian newspaper.

He famously delivered the most eloquent indictment of the British press during a press conference at Conservative Party headquarters, on the 10th April 1995, the same day that the paper had published a damning front page story about him and the Saudi's:

"If it falls to me to start a fight to cut out the cancer of bent and twisted journalism in our country with the simple sword of truth and the trusty shield of British fair play, so be it. I am ready for the fight. The fight against falsehood and those who peddle it. My fight begins today. Thank you and good afternoon."

That evening a World in Action programme was broadcast by Granada TV that repeated the allegations and Aitken sued for libel.

Aitken's libel action collapsed in June 1997 (a month after he had lost his seat in the 1997 General Election) when the Guardian and Granada produced evidence countering his claim that his wife, Lolicia Aitken, paid for a stay at The Ritz Hotel in Paris when it transpired that his wife had been in Switzerland at the time.

He was subsequently charged and convicted of perjury in 1999 and was sentenced to eighteen months in prison. Whilst in prison he "rediscovered the Bible" and became a student of Christian theology at Oxford University. He was released after serving just seven months.

Bless Jonathan. He was kind enough to reply to some correspondence I sent him by telling me, "I am afraid I am not a suitable person to contribute to your book because in terms of worldly success my life has been a great failure." His humility is indeed touching.

Top yourself in mysterious circumstances

Maybe you are caught so red-handed that maintaining your innocence is pointless. Maybe you are so unloved that there is nowhere to run to and hide. Maybe you are too worried about faking a serious illness because you may actually fall ill in the process and you cannot bear acting out the suffering. It may be easier to just go straight to the end-game and top yourself in

$ecret Habit$ of $ucce$$ful Ba$tard$

mysterious circumstances; it will save all that grief.

If you are a fat old bastard with a yacht, why not go and spend a fortune in luxurious marina casinos and just jump off it when you are ready. It was good enough for Lord Robert Maxwell.

If you have a coronary heart condition, which let's face it is a good chance if you have been living the high life, just let it take you to the next world while you stay at your ski chalet in Aspen Colorado. It worked for Kenneth Lay.

You could on the other hand, make it look like you topped yourself and leave your clothes on a beach like John Stonehouse did. You could, if you are really lucky, just overdose on drugs, drink, food and sex. Become the next Elvis Presley and remind yourself that whatever happens, in many people's minds still to this day - Elvis Lives.

It seems somehow appropriate that I end this book on death, albeit at your own hand if needs be. I want you to enjoy your life and make it richer for yourself and those around you. It helps me to remember that death awaits us all, that this is a short innings and we must all make the very most of that we possibly can.

Good luck, not that you will need it.

;-)

$ecret Habit$ of $ucce$$ful Ba$tard$

Appx 1 – Successful Bastard's Bingo

Successful Bastard's Bingo

Showing off about how clever they are	Getting unreasonably impatient about something	Giving orders to people	Failing to do what they promised	Talking about themselves at length
Changing the rules so that they can win	Moaning about how someone else has let them down	Being rude to someone	Lying through their teeth	Being nasty and rude to someone
Only worrying about themselves	Blaming someone when it isn't their fault	Creating an argument for no good reason	Stealing someone else's ideas	Not caring about a person's Feelings
Showing off about what they have as possessions	Failing to forgive someone who made a mistake	Throwing an object at someone	Encouraging someone to cook the books	Letting someone down badly
Not doing something they promised to do	Picking on someone weak and powerless	Making a decision despite having no grounds to make it	Taking a massive risk	Interrupting people mid-sentence

Appx 2 – Measuring people on the Bastardometer

I have developed a simple questionnaire based model for identifying how much of a bastard you are. The Bastardometer will allow you to identify how frequently a person displays the key characteristics of a Successful Bastard.

You can have fun measuring yourself and others and get a formal certificate from the Society of Successful Bastards that will provide a permanent record of just how much of a bastard you are.

Simply use your web browser to access the web-site below and an interactive tool will guide you through the process:

www.successful-bastards.com

There will also be opportunities whilst you are there to get handy extra tips, communicate with other like-minded people and to tell me about your own experiences of living in the world of successful bastards.

$ecret Habit$ of $ucce$$ful Ba$tard$

INDEX

$ecret Habit$ of $ucce$$ful Ba$tard$

$ecret Habit$ of $ucce$$ful Ba$tard$

$ecret Habit$ of $ucce$$ful Ba$tard$

$ecret Habit$ of $ucce$$ful Ba$tard$